SALVAGE

CONFLICT
in the SHADOWS

The Nature and Politics of Guerrilla War

CONFLICT
in the SHADOWS

The Nature and Politics
of Guerrilla War

by James Eliot Cross

Doubleday & Company, Inc.
Garden City, New York
1963

Library of Congress Catalog Card Number 63–11227
Copyright © 1962, 1963 by James Eliot Cross
All Rights Reserved
Printed in the United States of America
First Edition

I first met James Cross in London, in 1943, when we were both in the business of special operations—the business of supporting the anti-Nazi resistance in Europe. By 1943, the British Special Operations Executive was a professional outfit (though the long-established British secret intelligence service considered SOE an amateurish upstart) while the Special Operations branch of the Office of Strategic Services, where Jim Cross and I wound up, was just learning the ropes.

They were fascinating ropes to learn. One lesson from that wartime experience seemed very clear. Given the proper circumstances, internal resistance can be an extraordinarily effective military instrument.

No less an authority than Dwight D. Eisenhower said after V-E Day that the anti-Nazi resistance in Europe was worth more than twenty divisions to the Allied cause. Yet until very recently, this wartime lesson in the impact of the war from within was forgotten in the West. If one reviews postwar history, it is astonishing that this should be so.

For the lesson was not forgotten in the East. On the contrary, in the last twenty years, guerrilla warfare has been a tool of Communist pressure and expansion, from Cuba to China, from Greece to South Vietnam. This was long before Nikita Khrushchev, in his famous speech of January 6, 1961, officially enshrined "just wars of national liberation" as the chief instrument of Communist expansion.

Yet only since John F. Kennedy took office has guerrilla warfare become in official Washington what the British dons call "a topic"—something sufficiently interesting to be talked about.

Nowadays, of course, "counterinsurgency" is very much a topic. For the hard lesson has at last been learned. Khrushchev meant exactly what he said in his January 6 speech. And what he said amounted to this: The Communists intend to use their highly refined technique of guerrilla warfare to "bury" our kind of civilization, under the umbrella of mutual thermonuclear terror.

Fortunately, in the long intervening years when the nature of the Communist guerrilla threat was misunderstood or disregarded, a small band of criers in the wilderness recognized the threat and made it their business to study and understand the nature of guerrilla warfare. One of these is Jim Cross. Since those wartime days, Jim Cross has gone on to become a leading authority on unconventional war. This book represents a distillation of years of study, thought, and experience.

As Mr. Cross points out, a guerrilla movement can become effective only under certain conditions. One requirement is the support, or at least the passivity, of the mass of the population. Another is powerful external support. A third is the conviction of ultimate victory.

In certain circumstances, Communist power and the Communist mystique supply these requirements. Not in all—Communist-inspired "wars of national liberation" have failed more often than they have succeeded. But one thing at least seems certain. The American commitment in South Vietnam, which has already cost billions of dollars and many American lives, is only the beginning of the story, not the end. The long struggle to contain Communist expansion which stretches ahead is more likely to take the form of this special, essentially political form of warfare than all-out thermonuclear war. Thus anyone seriously interested in the realities of the struggle will be amply rewarded for reading this admirable book.

Washington, D.C.   STEWART ALSOP
December 1962

For nearly a decade the chief military interest and concern of most Americans has been the awesome possibility of thermonuclear war. Today the American people are increasingly concerned by a threat at the opposite extreme of the spectrum of military violence. This is the problem of subversion, irregular warfare, and externally incited revolutions in the underdeveloped nations. Many of the weaker states of the free world find their progress toward peaceful development and modernization impeded, and their very existence threatened by insurrections which are either Communist-inspired and -directed or which give the Communists new and improved opportunities to seize power.

The United States is providing vast amounts of aid and has made broad treaty commitments to assist and protect many of these nations while they work their way toward political stability and economic health. Hence, Americans have a deep and urgent interest in meeting the challenges presented to these states by the unconventional aggression the Communist states are waging today.

This aggression is a complex undermining of government capability, social cohesion, and normal economic processes. It involves political, psychological, and economic agitation, as well as military activity.

As is often the case, popular attention in this country has focused on the most violent and dramatic aspect of the effort; that is the military, and for the most part this takes the form of guerrilla warfare.

There are now available a large number of excellent studies on the techniques and tactics of guerrilla war. Mao Tse-tung and other Communist writers have propounded their doctrines of revolutionary war, in which guerrilla operations play a large role. Still there seem to have been relatively few Western efforts to review modern unconventional warfare as a whole; to examine, even in general terms, the political, economic, and military context in which most guerrilla warfare takes place.

This book is an effort to do that. The purpose here is to look at the circumstances under which restive and changing regions become particularly vulnerable to subversion, insurrection, and revolution, at the forms these upheavals are likely to take, and at some of the measures which have proved effective in easing the tensions that make for turmoil and political collapse. If the book can assist the reader in forming or clarifying his thoughts on the nature and scope of this form of warfare, it will have served its purpose.

I want to express my sincere thanks to my wife who encouraged me to undertake this book and assisted throughout, as well as to my friends and colleagues who advised and helped me.

First, there is Brigadier General Sidney F. Giffin, USAF (Ret.), who, having the office next to mine, heard the birth pangs, chapter by chapter, and was unfailingly helpful—and patient. Stewart Alsop made a number of constructive suggestions and has been good enough to write a foreword. Others who have read and commented on the manuscript are: John A. Bross, James E. King, Jr., Franklin A. Lindsay, the Hon. Garrison Norton, Kermit Roosevelt, Bruce G. Sundlun, and Charles W. Thayer.

During the past year I was fortunate to be a member of a discussion group on unconventional warfare at the Council on Foreign Relations. I am indebted to the members of that group and to its chairman, Franklin Lindsey, as the meetings were unfailingly stimulating and greatly helped me to arrange my own thoughts.

The Institute for Defense Analyses, of which I am an associate, made available to me the time and facilities that permitted me to write this book. I am deeply grateful. Needless to say, opinions expressed herein are mine and do not reflect an official viewpoint of the Institute. I must also thank the library and secretarial staffs of the Institute.

Finally, it must be evident that with such excellent advisers and aides any errors herein are mine and mine alone.

James Eliot Cross
International Studies Division
Institute for Defense Analyses
Washington, D.C.
October 8, 1962

"Now a word about national liberation wars. . . .

"Can such wars occur in the future? They can. . . . But these wars are popular uprisings. In other words, can conditions be created in which people will lose their patience and rise in arms? They can. What is the attitude of the Marxists toward such uprisings? A most positive one. . . . The Communists fully support such just wars and march in the front rank with the peoples waging liberation struggles."

Chairman Nikita Khrushchev, January 6, 1961.
Report on the Moscow Conference of November 1960.

"The Free World's security can be endangered not only by a nuclear attack, but also by being slowly nibbled away at the periphery, regardless of our strategic power, by forces of subversion, infiltration, intimidation, indirect or non-overt aggression, internal revolution, diplomatic blackmail, guerrilla warfare or a series of limited wars.

"In this area of local wars, we must inevitably count on the cooperative efforts of other peoples and nations who share our concern. Indeed their interests are more often directly engaged in such a conflict. . . . We need a greater ability to deal with guerrilla forces, insurrections, and subversion."

President John F. Kennedy, March 28, 1961.
Special Message to Congress on the Defense Budget.

Contents

I

The Guerrilla Epidemic

The world today can look back at some thirty years of widespread and virtually continuous political revolution. Probably more governments have come into being, passed through drastic change, or ceased to exist than in any comparable period in history. Certainly a larger proportion of the world's population has been involved in and aware of these changes than was ever the case in earlier days.

These revolutionary transformations have taken many forms. Some have been violent, while others, considering their magnitude, have been remarkably peaceful. Many changes have been long foreseeable, in general terms at least, for they are the almost inevitable result of social development and economic growth. Some, like the wholly peaceful emergence of the Philippines as an independent republic, had been planned for many years in advance. But most of the changes, and this includes many of the most important ones, are the direct results of the turmoil and dislocations of two world wars.

Leaving aside the defeat and occupation of the Axis powers, the political impact of World War II was first and most directly evident in the nations of Eastern Europe where the presence of Russian military forces protected and assured success to the series of revolutions that carried that region into the Soviet bloc.

Many other changes resulted directly and clearly from the course and conduct of that war. The struggle sapped the strength

and authority of the colonial powers and simultaneously sharpened the determination of the leaders and peoples in the colonies
to achieve rapid, if not immediate, independence. Hence the
continuing emergence over the postwar years of a host of new
nations, most of them underdeveloped economically and woefully inexperienced politically, but nevertheless determined to
make out on their own.

During the same period the course of world events has heavily
strained many other nations, long independent but possessed of
weak economies or uncertain governmental structures. Many of
these countries have also experienced drastic political changes.

This general instability has been sharply increased by the continuing efforts of the Communist nations to expand the influence
and control of Communism in the underdeveloped areas of the
world. In form these offensives have ranged from the flagrant
military aggression in Korea to the legally correct efforts to provide aid and guidance to such states as Egypt and Indonesia. The
Communist efforts have further disturbed already highly unstable situations and greatly increased the likelihood of violence
in any changes which do take place.

In a nation or society with strong political traditions and a
popular understanding of the values of peace and order, a change
of leadership may not affect the structure of the government itself, and even substantial changes in the pattern of government
are not likely to disrupt the pattern of the society. An election,
possibly rowdy and bitter, but essentially non-violent may be
enough to do the job. Through a large part of the world, however, such traditions and controls do not restrain either the leaders who may be thrown out or the rival leaders and populace who
hope to do the throwing. The result is repression and then frequently rebellion and tumult.

In cases where the military forces of the nation or a significant
part of them join the rebels there may be a palace revolution or
coup d'état; the sort of switch we associate traditionally with

Latin America, but which is now practiced a good deal more widely. Nasser in Egypt, Kassim in Iraq, and the present military government in South Korea all came to power by this route.

If the rebels lack sufficient military power to gain a quick victory the result may be a civil war of the sort that scarred Spain when Franco's thrust for power ran into unexpectedly solid opposition, and the nation went through three years of conflict that still haunts its people today.

Usually, however, rebellious citizens have neither the talent nor the means to organize an army that can meet the government forces in conventional battle and thus support a direct bid for power. They can only nibble away at the strength of the government by subversion and irregular attack. Of necessity they become slow-motion revolutionists.

Anyone setting out to study or discuss rebellions of this sort at once runs into semantic difficulties, for many terms are used which, while largely synonymous, have come to mean different things to different men. For our purposes the simplest definitions are certainly the best. Rebellion, uprising, revolt, insurrection, and insurgence all describe a rising against authority and according to Webster are largely interchangeable. They will be so used here. Clearly, these activities do not create a revolution, unless and until they are successful, but a revolutionist, seeking to make a revolution, is equally clearly a rebel or an insurgent. Subversion is also an effort to overthrow authority, but usage has given the word a less violent connotation than the others.

The violent and semimilitary forms and phases of rebellion have produced some confusing terms as well. Armed men who fight against government authority, but who do not or cannot operate as conventional soldiers, are variously known as irregulars, guerrillas, or partisans. Again, these terms are largely interchangeable, although partisan has been more generally associated with bands of men who work with, and in support of, conventional troops in a time of large-scale and acknowledged

war. In the same sense, resistance forces are usually considered
irregulars or guerrillas who are fighting to discomfort or expel
invading armies which have conquered and occupied their native
land.

During the past few years guerrilla has become a badly over-
worked word, for it has been generally applied to almost all
forms of violent and armed revolt against government authority.
Hence, there has been a tendency to refer to all forms of sustained disorder and rebellion as guerrilla warfare, and the term
guerrilla has come to cover every sort of armed miscreant from
bandit to devoted political revolutionary. In large measure this
broad usage of the term stems from the government authorities
who are threatened by the activity of the irregulars. In the postwar guerrilla fighting in Malaya, the government regularly referred to the rebels as terrorists, and during the Philippine insurrection, forty-five years earlier, we described the insurrectionists
as ladrones or thieves.

Often, of course, there is considerable truth in the government's assertion, for it is probable that over the centuries more
irregulars have been led on by lust for loot than love of country
or principle.

No military commander ever received greater support and assistance from friendly guerrillas than did the Duke of Wellington in his Spanish and Portuguese campaigns, but we find his
military secretary writing that "Many of them (the guerrillas),
under the pretense of patriotism and of serving against the
enemy, became regular freebooters and subsisted on the pillage
of the country. . . . While some of them kept alive the spirit of
resistance and the feeling of hatred against the French, others
compelled the inhabitants to look to the French for protection;
for the inhabitants would at length prefer the systematic pillage
and regulated contributions of the enemy to the wasteful, ca-
pricious, uncertain, and merciless plundering of their own coun-

trymen."[1] Lawlessness increases during any period of serious unrest, and the luckless victim of violence is not prone to analyze good and bad motives too carefully.

Guerrilla operations can and do take many different forms, but it is important to note that the ultimate objective of the rebellion directly and sharply affects the courses the guerrilla leader may follow in seeking his victory. In an article written some fourteen years ago,[2] Mr. Julian Amery distinguished clearly between what he called the "have" and "have not" resistance movements: those movements which seek to restore an earlier political order, and those which have no interest in previous structures and seek to set up wholly new systems of government.

Most of the resistance movements of Western Europe during World War II fought to overthrow the German occupation and to regain something like the *status quo ante bellum*. Mikhailovitch and the guerrillas under his command in Yugoslavia considered themselves a part of the Royal Yugoslav Army, forced into irregular operations after the military defeat by the Germans in 1941. As such they tried in their campaign to preserve what they could of the old social and political order. Tito, on the other hand, had quite different aims. He shared Mikhailovitch's desire to throw out the Germans, but he was equally determined that the Royal Yugoslav Government should not return to power. He sought to create a new government himself; a government based on a wholly new political and social structure. Hence, he welcomed rather than feared the disruptive and destructive changes of war.

A guerrilla campaign can therefore be essentially protective, as was, for example, the Norwegian resistance in World War II,

---

[1] *Supplementary Dispatches, Correspondence and Memoranda of Field Marshal Arthur Wellesley, Duke of Wellington, K.G.* John Murray, 1860, Vol. 7, p. 450.

[2] "Of Resistance," *The Nineteenth Century and After*, March 1949, p. 138.

or it can be innovative, as were the Cuban insurrections against
Spain in the late nineteenth century and against the Batista
government in the nineteen fifties.

Sometimes this protective-innovative distinction can be seen
in different periods of insurrection in a single country. Almost
four hundred years ago, when Britain's Elizabethan generals
sought to extend their control over Ireland beyond the Dublin
Pale, the Irish leaders like Tyrone fought a guerrilla war against
them to defend a crude but long-established tribal system of
their own. In this century when the Sinn Fein brought the
Irish struggle to a climax through a use of guerrilla tactics, the
British rule had lasted so long that the Irish leaders had no practical political pattern or system to adhere to. Their campaign
was a purely anti-British offensive, and after victory they had to
fight a bloody civil war among themselves to determine the positive system for which they had struggled through the years.

With the notable exception of the French OAS activities in
Algeria and metropolitan France, almost all recent insurgent
campaigns have been innovative. Their leaders seek to destroy
an established order and to create something wholly new. This
is true, not only of Communist-led and -dominated movements,
but of essentially non-Communist efforts like that of the FLN in
Algeria, the Mau Mau in Kenya, and the EOKA in Cyprus.
Therefore, although comparisons between such movements and
campaigns like those of the French Maquis, the American Plains
Indians, and the Portuguese Ordenanza of Napoleon's day may
prove illuminating and useful in helping to understand current
conflicts, it must be remembered that the objectives and consequently the operating philosophy of all these forces may have
been substantially different.

Insurrection takes on another dimension when the insurgents
are encouraged and supported by the government of another
state. Inciting rebellion then becomes a technique of foreign
policy and a form of unconventional aggression by one national

government against another. Since this sort of unacknowledged and irregular attack is not aggression in the classical sense of the word, it is difficult to demonstrate to international tribunals and to the world at large that aggression is indeed taking place, and as a result effective forms of defense and retaliation are hard to determine and carry out. This is unconventional warfare as we are seeing it waged today.

Attacks of this sort are certainly nothing new in the world, for stirring up trouble in the territory of neighboring states is an ancient political pastime. Encouraging rebellion and civil war by supporting and guiding disaffected minorities has always been a temptingly easy way of making trouble and gaining political objectives. For example, the government of France complicated and enlivened British politics for well over a century by supporting the Stuart claims to the British crown, and that policy was not wholly different in its tactics and objectives from the infinitely more extensive efforts that the Communist leaders are pursuing in most of the underdeveloped countries today. The significant fact is that unconventional warfare in the form of subversive attack and guerrilla activity is now a key element in a worldwide drive for power and domination.

There are a number of insurrections taking place today with the help of neighboring governments in which Communism is not an immediate issue. The Congalese-aided rebellion against the Portuguese in Angola is a case in point, but most of the risings which directly and seriously concern American policy-makers today are inspired, guided, and fed from behind the borders of the Communist states.

On January 6, 1961, Khrushchev made his famous speech in which he announced that the Soviets would lend their support to wars of national liberation, or unconventional wars within the nations of the free world. This made a matter of public record a policy which the Soviet Union had long been following, and Khrushchev did not spell out in detail why this policy was desirable and potentially fruitful for the Soviets. It is important to examine and understand why this line, at this time, seems so appealing and promising for the Communist world.

It is not that modern technology has given the rebel guerrilla military advantages over his more conventional opponent. Technological advances have certainly changed the nature of guerrilla war, as it has that of all warfare, but the shift in relative advantage has been slight and has probably worked in favor of the conventional government soldier. Through history the guerrilla has been materially weaker than his enemy, and this is still the case today.

Obviously one major factor is the existence and organization of national Communist parties throughout the underdeveloped regions. There is no denying that the small but disciplined cadres of the national Communist parties are extremely adaptable and effective tools of politics, and this is proving particularly true in the underdeveloped areas where shifts of attitude toward political authority and traditional ways are likely to be the most sudden and explosive. These groups are well suited to identify with, and act on, popular grievances and to stir up considerable unrest even where the grievances are not pressing or serious. In most of the underdeveloped regions there have been plenty of ready-made grievances with which they have worked. These rebellious minorities have demonstrated that by exacerbating and exploiting existing tensions, they can, over time and with adequate assistance and support, build an aggressive military opposition that may finally destroy the government's ability to govern and thus reduce the country to a welter of confusion and civil war.

But equally important is the fact that Communism has long been advertised by its leaders as the wave of the future. An essential element in the appeal it holds for its followers in all parts of the world is the belief that Communism must inevitably grow and spread to dominate all nations and all men. The inexorable process of "liberation" of all capitalist states is key to the whole concept. Since no true believer can accept the notion that Communism as a world movement will be rolled back, it must, like the wave it purports to be, move constantly forward. To lose momentum would mean collapse and disintegration.

The Communists have long recognized and anticipated that this process must inevitably involve violence and war. In the pre-nuclear age this cheerful prospect did not, in the abstract at least, trouble any orthodox Communist, and apparently it still does not greatly disturb some of the Chinese Communist leaders. However, even the most cursory look at the appalling consequences of an all-out thermonuclear conflict makes it clear that there can be no ultimate winner, and this conclusion is just as evident in Moscow and Peiping as in the West. The forward momentum called for by Communism's creed must therefore be assured by some lesser form of conflict; preferably by the form least likely to lead to escalation into an unprofitable, and almost certainly disasterous, holocaust.

The Communist search for a reasonably safe brand of aggression has been going on now for some sixteen years.

The absorption of the Eastern European states did not give much guidance for future operations, as that was really a matter of digesting politically what had already been eaten militarily by the Red Army. The sharp Western reaction to the aggression in Korea made it clear that open attacks of that sort were no answer.

It is worth noting, however, the Chinese decision to dub as volunteers the men of the army they sent to fight in Korea did provide a legal loophole which, when officially unchallenged by the United Nations, permitted all the powers involved to avoid an escalation and expansion of the war. It seems pretty clear that Khrushchev had the advantages of that distinction well in mind when he threatened to send volunteers to the aid of Egypt during the Suez fighting in the autumn of 1956.

In Malaya and in the Philippines the Communist parties made strong bids for power through guerrilla-type campaigns.

Both failed, but they failed after forcing the governments of both countries to fight long, hard, and almost ruinously expensive campaigns during which the economies of the countries were grievously damaged and the normal patterns of life seriously disrupted. These campaigns failed for two reasons. The governments had adopted wise, imaginative, and farsighted policies and programs to counter the attack, and in both instances the geographical situation had prevented the Communist states from providing the rebels with meaningful amounts of material support.

This last difficulty underlined the lesson on unconventional war which the Communists had learned earlier in Greece. There, in the years immediately after the war, Communist-led guerrillas had received massive aid and reinforcement from across the Yugoslav and Bulgarian borders and were well on the way to overthrowing the government by the spring of 1948. Then, following Tito's break with Moscow, the Greek-Yugoslav border was closed, and the guerrillas in Greece, deprived of well over half their support and barred from their most valuable bases, became gradually weaker. The Greek government was able to assume the offensive, and the threat of a Communist take-over by guerrilla action was past.

The evident conclusion of these campaigns was that unconventional offensives built around guerrilla operations and mounted against reasonably responsive and competent governments have little chance of gaining national victory unless they receive sustained and large-scale support across a contiguous border and can look to the Communist side of that border as a sanctuary and base as well as a source of supply. These were the conditions under which the Vietminh were able to defeat the French in the long Indochina war, and it is precisely this situation which obtains, at this writing, in South Vietnam.

It is safe to say that even the most adept guerrilla leader can only win his way to power unaided if the government opposing him is spectacularly unimaginative, weak, and unpopular. This was certainly true of Batista's regime in Cuba which fell to pieces as Castro's movement gained momentum.

Still, a Communist reviewing the guerrilla warfare campaigns of the past twenty years which have failed to gain power will find a great deal in the balance sheet to please him and much that augers well for the future. The cost of these failures has been relatively light. Materially it comes to stocks of obsolescent or easily replaceable light weapons, many of which were either captured from the enemy or obtained locally. The personnel losses were certainly more serious, for they included many of the old party members, heading the cadres around which the national parties have been built. Still, these men are ultimately replaceable and the numbers involved were seldom large. The operating philosophy of the Communist parties conveniently reconciles successive local defeats with ultimate over-all victory, so these badly mangled parties have never died out. As I mentioned above, the governments found their victories infinitely more expensive to achieve. Disproportionate amounts of trained manpower, funds, and economic resources which they could ill afford to waste had to be thrown into the struggle, and normal national development was seriously hampered and delayed. In short, it was shown conclusively that even in an ultimately abortive guerrilla campaign a relatively small number of ill-equipped men could tie up even an efficient government for a considerable period of time.

Then too, it should not be forgotten that the techniques of unconventional and guerrilla warfare can be effective not merely against the target nations whose populations are already troubled and uncertain, but they can also have a divisive and corrosive influence on the stronger nations of the free world. After forty years of living on the same planet as the Soviets the nations of the earth have become accustomed and almost inured to Communist interference in their domestic affairs. Shenanigans which would well nigh provoke war between two non-Communist states become almost routine and, paradoxically, somehow less reprehensible when perpetrated by a Communist power. This "boys will be boys" attitude is a major reason why it is so difficult to mobilize international opinion and action to counter Communist unconventional offensives.

The disagreements and disputes within alliances and in international bodies over whether and what sort of action is required to meet any given situation can create serious stresses and strains, and overt action by any one power to intervene and assist a seriously threatened state takes on a stigma wholly disproportionate to that attaching to the original aggression. Should the present Soviet and Chinese policies succeed in increasing tensions and schisms among the nations of the free world, the opportunities for Communist subversion and disruption will increase immeasurably.

It is against these disagreeable possibilities that today's epidemic of unconventional warfare must be studied.

II

Troubled New World

During the early stages of the Communists' postwar search for safe and profitable ways to expand their areas of power they placed high hopes on the Communist parties of the industrialized nations of Western Europe. From the start it was clear that the parties in Britain and the United States would be of little use for anything other than sophisticated espionage, and at this they proved disconcertingly adept, but in France and Italy the Communist parties had large popular followings, and the disruption and destruction of the war had been severe. There things looked a good deal more promising, and there were reasonable grounds for the Communist leaders to think they might come to power through a more or less legal use of the electoral process.

These hopes soon proved illusory. The Communists lost the Italian election of 1948, which was their great opportunity in that country. They have always commanded an impressive popular vote in France, and over the years they have staged some spectacular riots, but as that nation first recovered and then vastly increased her industrial prosperity the chances for a Communist victory at the polls faded away.

Further east, the Communist guerrilla campaign in Greece lost headway with the defection of Tito's Yugoslavia from the Soviet bloc in 1948, while in 1949 the Chinese Communists succeeded in gaining complete control of mainland China. Therefore, although Berlin continued to be a focal point of conflict, and promises to remain so for some time, it was entirely natural for the more general emphasis of the over-all struggle to shift away from Europe to what are rather invidiously known as the underdeveloped nations. These nations, in Africa, Latin America, and southern Asia, make up the most natural and tempting areas for Communist efforts at expansion and take-over. Many of them are tailor-made targets for Communist infiltration and subversion, and a large number of them are topographically and climatically well suited to guerrilla operations.

Over the past few years events have given the American citizen quite an extensive education on these parts of the world. The birth pangs and growing pains of the new nations have been vividly covered in the press, the purposes and early adventures of the Peace Corps have been amply illustrated, and the pros and cons of military and economic aid to these regions have been argued back and forth repeatedly in the Congress and in the public print.

For these reasons there is little point here in attempting a profound analysis of the underdeveloped areas and their many difficulties. It is worthwhile, however, to review a few of the factors that give these regions the dubious privilege of being the contested areas in a worldwide struggle and the scene of so much bitter guerrilla fighting today.

As I mentioned earlier, World War II and the far-reaching changes which followed it reduced some of these regions to a state of disorder bordering on chaos. As the colonial powers withdrew or were thrown out, the new indigenous governments which replaced them found themselves up against political, social, and economic problems which have strained them to their limits. Inevitably the situation appears compellingly tempting to aggressively minded outsiders and ambitious men within the unstable nations.

Other states, confronted by some of the same challenges and difficulties as the newly emerged nations, have enjoyed their independence for many years, but have not developed political and social structures designed to meet the problems that are pressing in on them today. Iran and Peru are sometimes cited as examples of countries in this situation. Political and financial power has become concentrated in the hands of a relatively small number of citizens at the top of the heap, and the lives of the vast majority of the population have been hardly affected by the technical and economic advances of the twentieth century. Reforms and development programs are now being pushed forward urgently in a number of these regions, but it will be some time before their impact can be widely felt. These societies and governments are inherently unstable, for their populations are all too obviously susceptible to revolutionary propaganda and subversion. Communist spokesmen find much of their political and emotional groundwork already laid for them.

Therefore underdeveloped countries are vulnerable to insurrection and unconventional attack both when their governments are too weak and inexperienced to meet popular needs and also when their regimes have become too stiff in the joints to respond in time to the demands of changing conditions. In the one instance ambitious revolutionaries are led on by the apparent ease of brushing aside a half-formed system; in the other by the frustrations of trying to influence and move an inert bureaucracy. Either way suits the Communists, who can spark and lead a revolt themselves or seek to capitalize on the confusion of a non-Communist revolution and end up on top when the changes are over.

The vulnerability of many underdeveloped nations to insurrection and guerrilla attack is greatly increased by their geography and by their primitive economies. Transportation systems are usually rudimentary at best. Railroads tend to be few and far between and not too efficient in any case. Roads, with the notable exception of a few stretches which are meticulously maintained as showpieces, are likely to be rare, poor, and in the back country little more than trails. In monsoon areas many of these last will be just about impassable for wheeled traffic during parts of each year. Of course, there are shining exceptions to these sweeping generalizations and to those that follow, but as a rule travel is difficult, and it follows that civil and military authorities are handicapped in exerting centralized control. In varying degrees rural communities tend to be isolated and self-sufficient in a way that has not been seen in Western Europe since the end of feudalism.

In some new nations such as the Congo virtually no government existed. The borders of the state had been arbitrarily set at a time when they had hardly been explored, much less adequately surveyed, and the determination had had little or nothing to do with the ethnic patterns that may already have existed. In the Congo the reversion to tribal war following independence was almost immediate, followed by a rough division based on competitive interests which still had little relation to the needs and interests of the region as a whole. In the Congo instance a national entity has only been re-established by the horses and men of the United Nations who have managed to put Humpty Dumpty together again in the controversial maneuvering and fighting which has gone on sporadically since 1961. Time alone will tell whether the stitches of these rather frenzied operations will hold the thin national shell in one piece. Tribal guerrilla war is still dangerously close beneath the surface and will remain there for a long time to come.

Under these circumstances it is only natural that xenophobia, or dislike and distrust of strangers, which afflicts all of us to some extent, is frequently evident and plays an important part in forming social and political attitudes. Tribalism, acute provincialism, and sometimes racism, are strongly felt and likely to be strongly shown. To the secluded citizen, the representatives and authorities of his own national government, coming from a strange and sometimes distant capital, may be just as alien and just as offensive as men appearing from the other side of the world.

Frequently rough and forbidding terrain is a major reason for the poor transportation and communications in these regions and further complicates the government's task in maintaining peace and order. Guerrilla war can and has been waged in every sort of climate and country, but there is no question that jungles, marshlands, and mountains are the ideal forcing beds for this activity, especially where the distances are great and the forces of law and order are small.

Rugged and inaccessible regions can provide guerrillas with the secure bases which T. E. Lawrence and the subsequent Communist writers on the theory and practice of guerrilla warfare have all pointed out are essential for success in these operations. In such bases or hideaways supplies may be cached, wounded men cared for, and some training for new recruits conducted. From such bases without great danger of interference by government forces guerrillas can work outward to conduct their offensives, strengthen their ties with and control over the local population, and gradually expand their areas of power through the country.

Isolated villages and settlements rarely have the strength, even if they possess the will, to resist coercion and direction from guerrillas operating in their vicinity. They must look to the national government to provide, or at the least to assist in, their protection. But the national government is often far away, so the protection provided is often too little and arrives too late.

The combined problems of an ill-informed and isolated population, difficult country, and inadequate transportation would be difficult enough for even the most experienced, enlightened, and well-financed government, but the governments of most of the underdeveloped states are not likely to fill this bill.

With independence, vast stretches of Africa have been Balkanized to form numerous new states, each with its own aspirations, vulnerabilities, and difficulties. Many of these nations are acutely short of educated men, trained and competent to manage governmental matters. The same problem exists for a number of Asian nations such as Laos, South Vietnam, and Indonesia, and this lack of experience is a major reason for instability and frequently erratic national performance. Those countries where a competent civil service has developed over the years or was trained before the colonial power departed are extremely lucky, for they have the skeleton of a body politic already formed. Unfortunately, this advantage is enjoyed by all too few.

Therefore, a usual policy is to hold on tight, make such improvements as can be organized and afforded, and hope that if conditions gradually improve the lid will stay on. In any situation where there are deep popular grievances and an aggressive body of would-be revolutionaries this isn't likely to be enough.

It is all too easy to see why the leaders of these nations often stumble and falter. Those who are aware of the magnitude of their problems are acutely aware of their need for material assistance and discrete guidance, but they are also determined to assert continually their independence and competence. This determination is certainly nothing new or strange. A hundred and seventy-five years ago, when we were a new nation, our leaders repeatedly emphasized our resolution to go it alone, and Washington's statement on this point in his Farewell Address was the cornerstone of our foreign policy up to the eve of the Second World War.

The leaders of the new nations have vivid and often somewhat exaggerated recollections of past frustrations as colonials of a foreign power. The leaders of underdeveloped nations which have been independent for many years or generations have a natural patriotic pride and are reluctant to face the fact that the political and social system they have evolved over the years may be inappropriate or inadequate to meet today's demands.

Both of these attitudes make for dangerous delays in acknowledging difficulties or shortcomings when they do become evident, and inept or undiplomatic advice, shouted from the sidelines by friendly outside states, may make the harassed leaders more reluctant than ever to make necessary changes in their programs.

Therefore, recurrent imbalance and inequities are bound to appear in the changing social and political structure of each nation. Each of these is a new potential vulnerability and a new opportunity for insurrectionists and ultimately for the Communists.

For nowhere is the situation really static. The old political, social, and economic structures are being torn apart, whether or not new ones are ready to take their place, and with these structures are going the accompanying cultural patterns which are now becoming increasingly outdated and inappropriate.

Even the most secluded and distant backwaters are being exposed to new ideas and new pressures which at the same time seem to be sinister threats to time-honored ways and wonderous opportunities to escape from long-resented limitations and restraints. More new ideas and material innovations, together with the emotional strains that go with them, have been introduced into these parts of the world in the past twenty years than in the past five hundred. The result is unsettling, to say the least.

While it may be permissible to generalize about the nature and background of the underdeveloped regions, it is wholly impossible to make generalizations about the ways in which modernization is affecting them. Each area differs historically and geographically from the others, and each is developing and growing in a different way and at a different rate of speed. The separate but interrelated processes of political, social, and economic evolution and modernization progress in their own way in each region. To try to determine an average performance or to arrive at a meaningfully uniform pattern of progress for regions as different as, say, northern Laos, Tanganyika, and the highlands of eastern Colombia is about as hopeless and as unprofitable as trying to find an average fingerprint.

As the varied cements which have held traditional societies together crumble and give way, each society must find and build on its own strengths and opportunities, and each one is in danger of succumbing to its own particular vulnerabilities, be they tribal enmity, religious conflict, class rivalry, or violently aggressive nationalism.

Unfortunately these vulnerabilities continue to appear throughout the early stages of economic growth no matter how well intentioned the government may be. In his book, *The Anatomy of Revolution,* Dr. Crane Brinton made a detailed and perceptive study of four great political upheavals; the American, the French, and the Russian revolutions, and the English revolution of the sixteen forties. He stated that these revolutions "were not born in societies economically retrograde; on the contrary they took place in societies economically progressive." He pointed out that misery and privation was not the primary triggering factor, and quoted Trotsky's comment "In reality the mere existence of privations is not enough to cause an insurrection; if it were, the masses would always be in revolt."[1]

Thus, the government of an underdeveloped country is likely to face its greatest strains and challenges during the period when its people are making the greatest strides in their early moves toward modernization. During this chaotic period it is extraordinarily difficult at the same time to assure a reasonable progress toward economic development and an improved standard of living, to maintain a satisfactory semblance of law and order, to work toward concepts of individual freedom and perhaps a moderately representative government, and to conduct foreign policies in keeping with the responsibilities and prerogatives of an independent nation.

While the underdeveloped nations gradually modernize themselves their most unstabilizing vulnerabilities will change in character. Their troubles, as they progress, will not so much stem from lack of experience and shortages of trained man and leaders as from the inevitable discrepancies that will show up between

[1] New York: W. W. Norton & Company, 1938; Revised Edition, New York: Prentice-Hall, 1952, pp. 33–34.

the reality of a modest rate of progress and the wholly unrealistic expectations of new standards of living and new ways of life that should somehow appear almost overnight.

For example, in some of the new African states such as the Congo there is a truly desperate shortage of lawyers to serve as judges and to maintain a system of courts. The resulting uncertainties, delays, and inequities give rise to exactly the sort of confusion and disaffection on which revolt thrives. On the other hand, in many somewhat more advanced societies a surfeit of lawyers develops. The law is widely considered to be a fashionable and desirable profession, and as a result more men are often trained in the field than the economy of their country can absorb. As a result the Communist Party of the country may draw many of its ablest and most dedicated recruits from the disappointed and disillusioned men who find that they cannot make a suitable living in their profession and blame the system for their failure. While a nation's political, social, and economic structure grows more complex, the inevitable childhood diseases of industrialization create aches and fevers which simply have to be lived through, for no one has found a way wholly to avoid them. The towns grow larger, swelled by countrymen who are not adjusted to the demands of urban life. Some old grievances are eased, but at the same time old privileges and comforting patterns and traditions fade away. Those in the population who feel themselves forced into unwelcome transitions and those who feel frustrated and limited by the form and rate of change create strands of tension within the body politic. These men are the potential rebels, the men who may become guerrillas, and the men who, short of that, may openly or secretly support others in insurrection against a government which they feel has failed to understand their needs and protect their interests in a strange, new, and bewildering world.

III

The Nature of Unconventional War

Ever since Julius Caesar sat down to write about his wars, military men have shown an overwhelming compulsion to produce books about their campaigns and adventures. Even Captain Bligh of the *Bounty,* after surviving the famous mutiny, wrote an almost convincing description of how it had looked from his point of view. There was such a spate of conflicting military memoirs after the Second World War that future historians will be able to find respectable authority for almost any version of events they wish to put forward.

The great guerrilla leaders down through the centuries have not been so communicative. This is partly because a good many of them never had the opportunity. Also, many of the best of them were illiterate. However, their twentieth-century successors have made up the difference. Rough and rugged memoirs of irregular fighting are now available by the score, and a number of insurgent leaders, notably T. E. Lawrence and Mao Tse-tung, have written careful analyses of the theory and practice of guerrilla warfare.

Perhaps because of the mass of colorful information available on the exploits and achievements of guerrillas, many Americans have developed some startling ideas about the capabilities and limitations of these forces. In general they tend greatly to exaggerate their prowess. Then, too, the exploits of some highly successful irregular fighters have become a part of the American folklore. Marion the Swamp Fox, Ethan Allen and his Green Mountain Boys, Mosby of Virginia, and the western scouts such as Davy Crockett are known to every schoolboy. A guerrilla in the popular image is brave, dedicated, wily, and hardy, a brilliant tactician and a dead shot. There is no question that an experienced guerrilla is a tough and ingenious character; otherwise he would not have lived long enough to gain his experience, but he rarely, if ever, measures up to those specifications.

It has already been pointed out that guerrillas are forced to operate and fight as they do because they are not strong enough to do battle organized as soldiers. The evolution of a guerrilla band into a military force able to fight regular troops on anything like even terms will be examined later on. Suffice for the moment to say that it is a long and arduous process. Here again the national folklore leads Americans to underestimate greatly the difficulties of the transition from one to the other.

The untrained New England farmers who fought at Bunker Hill were glorious exceptions to an almost universal law. So were the militia and backwoodsmen who made up much of Andrew Jackson's force that threw back the British offensive against New Orleans in 1815. Later on, the defense of the Alamo seemed to confirm the instinctive American feeling that brave men didn't need much training to perform well as soldiers, and there has been a tendency to forget or play down Von Steuben's struggles at Valley Forge to whip the Continental Army into shape as a true military force.

It is important to remember that in these three battles the Americans did not have to maneuver. They held a defensive position and picked off an enemy advancing directly against them, inflicting very heavy casualties on their brave but unimaginative foes. But we must also remember that at Bunker Hill the American irregulars were finally defeated, and at the Alamo they were wiped out. Defeats are still defeats, no matter how bravely and stubbornly fought. Their memory may inspire other men to greater efforts in later fighting, but in themselves they do not win wars and conquer countries.

Rebels who cannot count on more conventional forces moving up to relieve or support them must win their own fights as best they can. Their objective is to survive and after victory to lead a life more to their liking. T. E. Lawrence pointed out that Posterity was a chilly thing to work for. Hence, such rebels make a virtue of necessity and fight as guerrillas.

The guerrilla's weapons are almost always inferior to those of his enemy, although there have been some notable exceptions to this rule. The Plains Indians who were able to buy or steal repeating Winchesters were certainly better armed than the soldiers who fought against them with the issue Springfield carbine of the eighteen seventies. The Pennsylvania rifle had some real advantages over the British Brown Bess musket of Revolutionary days, and Robin Hood was almost certainly as handy with a long bow as any of the Sheriff of Nottingham's men. But usually the soldier has the better hardware.

The insurgent must fight with what he can get, make, or steal from his enemy. This gives the average guerrilla band a bewildering variety of firearms with a correspondingly difficult problem of finding spare parts and ammunition. No weapon is improved by life in a rain jungle or sandy desert, particularly when it is occasionally buried or hidden in a stream bed and at the bottom of a rice paddy. The guerrilla has little chance to practice with whatever weapon he does possess. This is due partly to his rather busy life, partly to the fact that he is often camped where the sound of firing would give his position away to the enemy, but mainly to the chronic shortage of ammunition which afflicts guerrillas everywhere.

The insurgents in South Vietnam, like the partisans in Poland and western Russia during World War II, have been able to set up small and crude arsenals, often underground, and these have turned out some rough but serviceable equipment, but they can do relatively little to ease the constant shortage. Weapons captured from the enemy or brought in from outside of the country when such support is available remain the most reliable sources of supply.

Food is often an equally serious problem and limitation. In the most literal sense, guerrillas must live off the country. Preserving anything other than staples such as rice and flour is difficult, particularly in tropical climates. Attempts to store up stocks of even the staples in areas always subject to enemy occupation and search is risky and not always practical. Then too, the overriding need of all guerrillas to retain mobility and flexibility makes it impossible either to carry bulky rations for any extended period or to count on reliable lines of supply to bring in rations as needed. As always, there have been exceptions, and where guerrillas have been able to count on sure supplies of food, they have been immeasurably strengthened.

For example, the Arab irregulars operating against the Turkish military forces in the Hejaz during the First World War were often provided with the tinned rations of the conventional British forces with which they were cooperating, and this gave them a mobility which dependence on available fresh meat would never have permitted. Lawrence wrote afterwards that the invention of bully beef had profited them more than had the invention of gunpowder. In his own experience he was unquestionably right. His guerrillas were remarkably fortunate in that they enjoyed free access to a coast where friendly sea power waited to help and supply them. The baking little Arabian ports on the Red Sea and, later in the war, the harbor of Aqaba, near what is now the southern tip of Israel, were beyond the reach of the Turkish military forces, and thus Lawrence enjoyed an unassailable refuge and an unassailable base. The first was the trackless desert to the east of the Hejaz, the other was the bounty and succor of the Royal Navy ships which moved at will off the coasts.

Incidentally, providing support of this sort for friendly guerrillas was no new task for the British Fleet. When the French armies of Napoleon were bogged down in their long and wearing struggle to suppress the Spanish guerrillas, ships of the Royal Navy cruised both the Mediterranean and Atlantic coasts of Spain, putting ashore munitions and provisions where the guerrillas most needed them.

But the Arabs and the Spanish guerrillas in the coastal areas were definite exceptions to the rule. Since the usual guerrilla cannot store or assure delivery of food, he must fill his daily needs from the region in which he operates. This means that he must receive a good part of his sustenance from the population, and if this is not freely given him he must take it.

In areas where the people are for the most part friendly to him, they will do their best to help, but often this is not the situation. Where the population is not enthusiastically on his side, he must pay well for what he takes or run the risk of further alienating them. Often the guerrilla does not have the money to pay for his food, and, if there is a general shortage, the villager may not have the food to sell to him.

In short, the guerrilla cannot count on regular rations, and in more cases than not, he is badly fed and hungry a good part of the time. Traditionally, the hungry man fights well for he has something immediate to fight for, but over a period of weeks and months malnutrition can put him at a great disadvantage against the regularly supplied troops he is fighting.

In Malaya, where food was almost impossible to find in the jungle, hunger drove the guerrillas to come to the villages, and this set the pattern for much of the struggle. The British moved large numbers of civilians from the fringes of the jungle to new villages which could be defended, and, in consequence, they were able to reverse the traditional game and set ambushes for the guerrillas when the latter approached in search of supplies. This resettlement program, known as the Briggs Plan, was highly successful. The government of South Vietnam is working on a comparable program of defended villages today.

If food is a problem for the guerrilla, medical supplies and care of wounded is a far worse one. The uncertainty of obtaining supplies of any sort means that guerrilla bands can never be sure of adequate drugs for their ill and injured, much less suitable medical care for them. Units that must be constantly on the move and able to travel quickly and far if the conditions require it cannot be encumbered with invalids. Still, the morale of even the most fanatic insurgents will not bear up if wounded are simply abandoned, untreated, to the enemy as a matter of regular policy. Occasionally there is no alternative, but crude hospitals of a sort are usually set up, either secretly under the care of sympathetic members of the population or in remote areas where the danger of discovery and attack is the least. Inevitably these arrangements leave a lot to be desired. They divert men and facilities which the guerrillas can ill spare from other activities. Every wounded man becomes a relatively immobile hostage to fortune, and at the best, the care he receives will be vastly inferior to that of any of his enemies who may be wounded. The guerrilla knows this, and, consciously or not, it is bound to affect his attitude and his actions.

In this connection it is interesting to note that Tito's guerrilla forces in Yugoslavia were able to evacuate well over ten thousand of their sick and wounded to American and British hospitals in Italy during the last two years of World War II. This greatly improved the combat effectiveness, mobility, and morale of the fighting men.

To counterbalance these handicaps guerrillas must develop and exploit three potential advantages. The first is greater mobility than the conventional military forces opposed to them. The second is a detailed and intimate knowledge of the countryside where the fighting takes place. Being native to the battlefield, the

guerrillas are likely to know it better than the soldiers who enter
the region to restore order. The third needed advantage is a better
intelligence service than that of the government forces, and this
must include a high level of security as to their own plans and
movements.

Virtually every successful guerrilla movement has possessed
these advantages, and every writer on guerrilla war has emphasized their importance. Correspondingly, successful counterguerrilla operations have invariably been based on carefully
planned and conducted efforts to deprive the rebels of one or
more of these assets.

In guerrilla war greater mobility does not imply greater ab-
solute speed, in the sense that one race horse is faster than another. It means that one side can move throughout all parts of a
region with greater ease and facility than the other; that it can
move on shorter notice, with less fanfare and consequent loss of
secrecy. It is the ability to concentrate forces, to strike an enemy,
and to withdraw to comparative safety before he has time to
organize an effective defense or a subsequent pursuit. Throughout the centuries the lightly armed and unencumbered guerrilla
has had this advantage over the more heavily equipped troops
who have sought to bring him to open battle and there destroy
him.

Even Caesar fretted at his impedimenta. The baggage of a
modern army is infinitely more burdensome. The appearance of
the internal combustion engine, and the truck that it moves,
proved too much of a temptation for many military planners and
organizers. The logistic tail of armies has grown yet longer and
heavier, and items of equipment which were previously considered desirable when available are now looked on as virtual neces-
sities. The conventional army in the field has become more and
more ponderous.

We Americans have probably carried this trend to its greatest extreme. We have made the uncomfortable business of fighting as comfortable as the nature of the thing permits, but we have paid a considerable price to do it, and the logistic tail that supports an American division in action amazes and appalls foreign officers. This solicitous attention to the fighting man is commendable, but when ours or any other army so conceived and so managed is up against a guerrilla enemy this munificence of supply can be a terrible handicap in conducting the business at hand.

With the appearance of the railroad, guerrillas learned that it was a threat in so far as it could move enemy troops to critical points of conflict far faster than they themselves could hope to travel. The same became even more apparent of the truck and the highway when they came on the scene. But the guerrillas' answer to these innovations was equally clear.

Highways and railroads with their constricted traffic produced more fruitful targets for ambush and sabotage than the guerrilla had ever enjoyed before, and his defense against the innovations was to move his bases, the wellsprings of his own operations, sufficiently far from these firmly fixed avenues that enemy troops would still have to come after him on their own legs. When guerrillas can draw their enemy away from his modern means of transportation, they have a chance to re-establish their traditional advantage of greater mobility, and their position is likely to be even better than it was before the development of these devices, for the enemy tends to become organizationally and emotionally accustomed to modern transport.

The appearance of the airplane, particularly the helicopter and the short takeoff and landing aircraft does materially alter the relative mobility of guerrillas and the regular forces to whom these items are available. Still, as we will see later, no wholly satisfactory doctrine for the use of special aircraft against guerrillas has been evolved to date, and the extent of their influence on operations of this kind is not yet fully clear.

The guerrilla derives obvious advantages from his superior knowledge of the countryside. Movement through rough terrain is always difficult, and it is infinitely more so when the ground is not known. Seeking out an enemy who knows the trails and the shortcuts, and who is familiar with remote hiding places, the most promising spots for ambushes, and the surest escape routes from any skirmish point, requires time and a disproportionate number of men. Forces which can dissolve into groups of two or three individuals and reassemble at a prearranged time and place can outmaneuver a force which must move and operate as a whole. In describing the efforts of the British Army to suppress the Boer commandos which operated as guerrillas under leaders such as De Wet and Smuts, the British *History of the War in South Africa* gives a vivid picture of the problem. "To arrest broken bubbles of mercury was a similar task to that which at this time confronted Lord Kitchener's troops. In all parts of South Africa they were called upon daily to get sight of the invisible, to crush the impalpable, and to surround nothing. The Commander in Chief clearly understood the nature of the problem before him. His heaviest blows, though they never failed to break up the enemy, did so into fragments so numerous and full of vitality that there was not a soldier in the British forces but wished that they might be reunited into a body worth finding, worth striking, or capable of being found and struck."[1]

Aerial photography and improved maps and communications can help an army faced with these difficulties, but the oldest solution, and the one that still seems the most effective, is to employ natives of the region who are willing to work with the government and to use them as scouts and guides, or to organize them into units which are better able to preserve the peace than

[1] *History of the War in South Africa 1899–1902*, compiled by direction of His Majesty's Government, Vol. 4, p. 198. London: Haust and Blackett, 1910.

even the most efficient outsiders. For example, Indian scouts were a recognized fixture in the American Army through most of the nineteenth century, and the Philippine Constabulary probably contributed more directly to the tranquillity of the islands during the years of American rule than did the regiments of the United States Army which made up the regular garrison. From their earliest days in India, the British raised and maintained battalions of indigenous troops, and, with the exception of the great Mutiny of 1857, these soldiers served well, both in keeping domestic order and in Britain's overseas wars.

When disciplined troops are available in sufficient numbers, when their equipment is suited to the task, and when the government cares nothing for popular opinion and support, an insurrection can often be stamped out by ruthless slaughter and subsequent terror. The world saw a hideous illustration of this technique in the Russian suppression of the Budapest rising in 1956. The Chinese Communists may have done very much the same thing in Tibet during the past three years, although hard evidence is still slim. To take an earlier example, Charlemagne executed forty-five hundred Saxon rebels in A.D. 782 and followed up with a military campaign which completely subjugated what remained of that people.

But when a government seeks to check an uprising and still retain the possibility for peaceful reconciliation and reconstruction after order is restored, indigenous, local support for and participation in its program is virtually essential. Certainly one of the most spectacular failures of alien military forces to restore this sort of order on its own was the British Army operation in Ireland from 1916 to the signing in 1921 of the treaty which made Eire an independent state. The Royal Irish Constabulary, which was perhaps the government's closest link to the local countryside and its people, was the target of a sustained assassination program by the rebels. This campaign and the government's policies produced a high rate of loss and resignation, and as the Constabulary's ranks thinned the government's ability to move against the rebels knowledgeably and effectively on the local level declined.

The British failure to gain the support of enough Irishmen, and their failure adequately to protect those who did support them, progressively weakened the government's chances of seeking out and destroying their foes. With the end of the World War in 1918, Britain was able to concentrate large military forces against the rebellion, but even in so small and open a country as Ireland, the Irish knew the ground as these newcomers could never hope to know it. The British efforts to create new special police forces such as the notorious Black and Tans merely hardened Irish bitterness without contributing much to government efficiency, and the insurrection moved forward to ultimate success.

In short, a government faced with a serious insurrection must have the means to gain and maintain virtually as close and intimate a knowledge of the territory and its people as the rebels possess. If the authorities cannot achieve this they will gradually lose control of the situation. Then they can either concede defeat, or, if they possess the means and the brutality, they can try the technique used by the Communists in Budapest. Some two thousand years ago, Tacitus described this sort of policy as making a wilderness and calling it peace. It is hardly a practical program for a state striving toward modernization and a growing measure of democracy.

The importance of local knowledge is, of course, a part of the over-all question of intelligence. In guerrilla war the military aspects of intelligence boil down to a few crucial questions for each side. The guerrillas, who cannot fight except on their own terms, must know enough of their enemy's plans and movements to avoid being trapped into battles which they cannot win, and enough of the enemy's weak spots to make their own strikes as safe and effective as possible. Conversely, the military authorities must gain enough information to find their foe and either to destroy him directly or to cut him off from the supplies and information which enable him to fight and live.

Then too, isolated units of government forces may well lack the strength to fight off attacks by concentrations of irregulars. The authorities must have accurate and prompt information of any significant concentrations and must be able either to avoid them or to concentrate their own forces in turn and seize the rare opportunity of destroying a large group of rebels at once. Failure to obtain or act on such intelligence can be disastrous, and this lesson has been repeated again and again through history. In the year A.D. 9, the Roman general Varus apparently ignored reports that the German tribes were massing against him and led his command in a march through the wilds of the Teutoburger Forest en route to their winter quarters. He was ambushed by overwhelming forces which took full advantage of the rough and thick terrain. Varus committed suicide, and Rome lost three legions in the worst military defeat of the Augustan age. So humiliating was this disaster felt to be that the three legions, the seventeenth, eighteenth, and nineteenth, were never reactivated throughout the long history of the Empire.

In 1755, the British General Braddock was similarly caught in the Pennsylvania forests by a mixed force of French soldiers and Indian irregulars. He was completely defeated, and the painful retreat of the survivors of the battle gave the young George Washington a rough and highly educational military experience.

Something over a hundred years later, after General Custer and his force had been annihilated on the Little Big Horn, it was determined that Bloody Knife, one of Custer's Indian scouts, had given him accurate advance information on the size of the hostile concentration of Sioux and Cheyennes that lay in front of him.

Nevertheless, he divided his force and rode on into battle with only five of the 7th Cavalry's twelve troops.

For some reason this lesson seems a singularly hard one to learn.

Maintaining good security, the certainty that the enemy has not infiltrated spies into the planning and conduct of one's own operations, is an essential part of intelligence operations in either conventional or guerrilla war. First-rate counterespionage or counterintelligence is critical for all guerrilla and counterguerrilla operations. Treason, or even the fear or the danger of it, can stop an insurrectionist movement dead in its tracks. There is no defense against it, for any important information that reaches the authorities gives them the very advantage they need to trap and destroy the militarily weaker guerrilla. The late President Magsaysay of the Philippines once told me that judiciously applied bribery was one of the most effective counterinsurgency weapons available to a government.

In both Malaya and the Philippines the authorities had great success with well-publicized programs which offered a virtually new start in life to a guerrilla deserter if he came in, surrendered, and gave full information about the group he had left. Additional rewards were offered if he was able to bring his weapon with him, with further bonuses for persuading friends or relations to surrender themselves and their guns. Further inducements were held out for guerrilla officers who could bring in their units with them and, in Malaya at least, there were rewards for men who brought convincing evidence that they had effectively put their noncom or officer *hors de combat* before coming in. Some of the evidence presented to prove this point was fairly grisly. Still, the authorities did all that they could to encourage surrenders, and generous rewards were usually paid out. As a result, the cohesiveness and effectiveness of the guerrilla groups deteriorated, their numbers dwindled, and the government gained invaluable information.

The quality and quantity of intelligence available to either guerrilla rebels or to the government depend directly on the relationship which the two sides enjoy with the population as a whole—the people among whom the battle is taking place. This relationship affects the course and outcome of the conflict in many ways. Guerrillas are directly dependent for their success and for their very survival on the support they receive from the citizenry. Mao's metaphor of the guerrillas being fish and the populace the sea in which the fish swim is probably the most celebrated statement of this fact, but all writers on guerrilla war have emphasized the point and all successful guerrilla leaders have realized it and acted accordingly. Supplies, recruits, and intelligence are the three essentials of any insurrection, and from the people these must come.

It is important to realize and remember that adequate support for a guerrilla movement does not necessarily mean the enthusiastic, voluntary backing of a large majority of the population. Indeed, in most underdeveloped countries the majority of the population has relatively little understanding of any but the most personal and immediate political issues, and many would have relatively little feeling one way or the other even if they did understand them. The active participation of a small number of people and the general apathy of the majority often provides all the popular support necessary to make a successful revolution.

T. E. Lawrence estimated that the Arab revolt would achieve its goal if 2 percent of the population made up an active striking force and 98 percent were passively sympathetic. Even in these figures he probably overestimated the requirements. Obviously guerrillas must assure that their operations are not given away in advance to the authorities, but in most instances the great mass of the population have only the most general idea of what is going on and are far from eager to involve themselves in any way. This is particularly true where there is any likelihood that the insurgents will discover and punish informers.

Where, during the early stages of a rebellion, the guerrillas are able to identify themselves with some popular issues, and where the government is either inefficient or corrupt, the insurgents are likely to gain sufficient tolerance, if not open approval, to thwart the authorities' efforts to suppress them. Even apparent approval may be far from wholehearted. To many rural people government above the village level has been something of a mystery, and they have tended to favor that regime which promises to be the least of several evils. No great emotional drives or questions of principle are involved. The primary aim of most of the population is to be left alone. Paradoxically, this desire is often coupled with a feeling that the government should, firstly, provide the means for improving the standard of living; secondly, it should not force changes and innovations at a pace or in forms which are not acceptable; and thirdly, it should provide military and economic protection for all concerned in this evolutionary process and do it without making heavy financial demands on the beneficiaries of its strength.

Since this political version of having one's cake and eating at just the desired rate of speed is clearly unattainable, there is bound to be some measure of discontent in nations going through difficult transitions. As we have seen, this includes nearly all the underdeveloped nations in the world. It is this inchoate and uncertain feeling that things ought somehow to be better that gives some insurgent guerrilla movements a measure of initial acceptance and hence the opportunity that they need to get started.

Once a dissident movement is underway, the citizens exposed to it must make one of two decisions. The first is whether or not they favor the rebellion so strongly and actively that they will go into the field to fight for it or will take almost equal risks to serve as active supporters and sources of intelligence and supply. Most people duck this alternative. The other decision is more demanding. In simplest terms this is to figure out whether or not the movement is likely to succeed in the long run, but, more immediately important, it is to determine whether the rebels will be able to enforce their demands in their immediate area.

The circumstances of guerrilla war force people to be remarkably opportunistic. Unless the government can guarantee the health and safety of its people, they must accommodate themselves to the demands of guerrillas who have the immediate power in the region they live in. These people become acutely aware of the importance of ending up on the right side. The temptation to defer judgment initially and then to jump on the right bandwagon at the appropriate time is compelling, for the penalties for guessing and acting wrongly are vividly evident. Therefore a guerrilla insurrection becomes serious for the government at the moment that a significant number of the population begins to take it seriously.

In short, the passive sympathy of which Lawrence wrote is often produced, not so much by conviction as by a desire to play it safe and to build a little credit with the resistance in case it comes out on top.

There have, of course, been truly remarkable revolts against tyranny, mounted in the face of what were obviously hopeless odds. Perhaps the most famous of these was the initial rising of the Spanish people in 1808 against the forces of Napoleon. Regions at opposite ends of the country exploded spontaneously within a few days of each other. French power was at first shaken and then firmly re-established, and the horror of the ensuing reprisals inspired Goya to the electrifying drawings which hang today in the galleries of the Prado. The extraordinary valor and ferocity with which the Jews of Warsaw defended the Ghetto against the German attacks in 1943 rings with the same quality of hopeless determination. Ironically the German youths of East Berlin showed a brief flash of the same spirit in the short-lived rising of June 17, 1953.

But in most instances, and to some extent even in the examples given above, the fight was carried by a small number and the remainder went along with them; perhaps because they sincerely wanted to, but certainly because at the time it seemed the best thing to do.

This last situation can be seen today in the contested areas of the world where the guerrilla wars are being fought out. Inhabiting a battlefield is trying and difficult at best. The people will provide support for that side which can punish them most seriously for disloyalty to its cause.

For all these reasons the statement that the population is supporting a guerrilla rebellion may be misleading. A better way of putting it is usually that the guerrillas have free access to the population and are therefore in a position to exert control. If guerrillas can reach members of the population more or less at will they are able both to propagandize them and to police them. Occasional or even frequent sweeps and checks by government forces can do little to revive or assure pro-government actions by a citizenry who know that as soon as the authorities are weakened or depart, they will again be subject to control and coercion by the guerrillas.

All insurgents face the problem of deciding the extent to which they can depend on the wholehearted and freely given assistance of the people and the amount of force, coercion, and terrorism they must use to assure that their needs are met. Ideally, of course, the less submission to pressure and the more voluntary enthusiasm the better, but a mixture of the two is almost invariably necessary. Mao plays down in his writings the use of terror as a guerrilla instrument of government, but it is clear that he counts on a degree of cooperation from potentially hostile elements of the people which must be based on either an intervention of divine providence on his behalf or compelling temporal pressure to force the laggards to see things in the right light. Since it is probably safe to say that the Almighty is not working as a propagandist for the Peoples' Republic of China,

Mao must have foreseen that terror and force would play a large role in creating the new China.

The Viet Cong guerrillas in South Vietnam have increasingly relied on terror and coercion to impose their will on the people of that country and to extract from them the support they require. There the mixture of carrot and stick used by the rebels has become more and more stick. So long as the guerrillas have the strength to swing the stick and access to people against whom they wish to swing it, they have little need to use a carrot to develop genuine enthusiasm in their cause. The people will continue to support the guerrillas because they have no alternative unless and until the government is able to protect them from guerrilla depredations and punishment.

IV

Urban Insurrection

Thus far we have taken a general look at unconventional war, particularly guerrilla war as it is being fought today in the back country of the underdeveloped nations. There are other forms of insurrection which deserve special attention. One of these is rebellion as it develops in the more thickly populated areas and in the cities. Urban disorder and revolt is not guerrilla warfare in the classic sense of the word, but it is closely related to it. The world is likely to see more of this sort of activity in the years to come, for urban violence is a natural symptom of political instability in areas where increasing industrialization has led to overly swift growth in the size of cities.

Even in the more backward areas there is an accelerating drift of population to the towns, and consequently there is an accompanying geographic concentration of political and economic power. A government may be able to survive and win out over a guerrilla movement which has established its authority over large sections of the countryside, but it is extremely hard to fight back against rebels who have gained control over cities, with the communications, transportation facilities, and commerce which center in them.

Waging war in the more civilized and built-up parts of a country presents peculiar problems and opportunities for both the rebel leaders and the government authorities, but the basic principles of operation change surprisingly little from those of the more wide-open guerrilla struggles in the back country. Each side still seeks to gain the active support of the population, and the contest is still primarily political rather than military.

Once more it is important to distinguish between traditional concepts and modern reality. Urban violence as we are seeing it today is an essentially different thing from the pitched battles which took place in cities during many revolutions of the past. This change is due primarily to the increased killing power of modern military automatic weapons, their effectiveness in the relatively constricted spaces of a city, and the difficulty which most rebels encounter in getting hold of and operating this sort of hardware.

Up until the end of the eighteenth century it was not unduly difficult for a mob to gain physical control of a city and to fight and defeat the regular troops of the city garrison in the process. Indeed one of the dangers that led the early Norman rulers of medieval England to strengthen the Tower of London was the realization that their Saxon subjects might take matters into their own hands and try to reverse the verdict of Hastings. During the French Revolution the mob of Paris was able to storm the Bastille and later the Tuilleries Palace and sweep all before them. A few years later, however, when Napoleon demonstrated the effectiveness of even muzzle-loading artillery against the same mob, the picture began to change.

Since that "whiff of grapeshot," the trend has run against open mass violence in cities as a successful revolutionary technique, and a government which can count on the loyalty of its troops and does not shrink from wrecking parts of the city in its effort to restore order can usually retain a margin of control.

As in all political developments there have been many apparent exceptions. Throughout the nineteenth century Parisians continued to tear up their streets to build barricades regularly and frequently. Governments were brought down, but the mobs were more the symbols of the discontent which forced the changes than the direct causes of them.

The short-lived Paris Commune of 1871 was the most serious and distinctive of those uprisings. On that occasion a strongly anti-monarchist faction representing various shadings of socialism did gain control of the city, set up a makeshift government, and then for several months fought a losing battle against the French Army. But there were very special circumstances which enabled the city's defenders to hold out for so long. France and her army were bewildered by the shattering defeats suffered the previous year in the Franco-Prussian War. The new and shaky government was in poor shape to assert the little authority it possessed. The rebel administration enjoyed the loyal support of the National Guard of the city, and this force was much aided by the desultory performance of the regular troops in the early phases of the battle. Hence, in its offensive to retake Paris and restore the authority of the national government, the army had to overcome moderately competent military forces which possessed and occupied the fortresses of the city's defense system. The French soldiers had the further handicap of having to fight and kill their own countrymen, knowing that their own Prussian conquerors still occupied much of eastern France.

In other cases, such as the draft riots of 1863 in New York, mobs have been able to assert temporary control over large sections of cities, but in many of these instances the government has been inhibited from bringing its full military force to bear by a desire to keep casualties to a minimum and to save as much as possible of the afflicted city from physical destruction.

On Easter Sunday of 1916, some two thousand members of the Irish Republican Brotherhood, armed largely with small arms which had been smuggled into the country, rose in revolt against the British authorities in Dublin. They seized control of several public buildings, but were crushed after holding out for several days against attacks by troops. After this defeat the Irish leaders limited themselves to guerrilla and semi-covert tactics which proved far better suited to their means and their ends.

There have, of course, been some remarkably stubborn and courageous efforts by untrained irregulars to contest possession of urban real estate with modern armies, but the record shows that they have little or no chance of success. The most familiar example today is probably the brief struggle of the Hungarian insurgents to hold Budapest against Russian armored divisions in 1956. The Republican defense of Madrid, particularly the University City area, during the Spanish Civil War of the thirties was a notable achievement, and the fact that it took Franco as long as it did to drive out the factory workers and hardly better trained international units which made up much of the defending force argues that the quality of his forces must have left a good deal to be desired.

The people of Paris rose against the Nazis during the last week of the German occupation in the summer of 1944 and were in control of at least a part of the city by the time General Leclerc's French armored division arrived in the capital. Still this does not provide an exception to the general rule of insurgent inferiority. The Germans were far more concerned by the approach of the Allied forces from the west and the slowly developing threat of the American Seventh Army moving north from the Mediterranean than by the attentions of the ardent amateurs in their midst. The Parisians' action was gallant but costly, and their heavy casualties were incurred in attempting to inconvenience an intruder who was already making for the door.

At about this same time the Polish Home Army rose in much the same fashion to hasten the Germans' departure from Warsaw, believing mistakenly that the advancing Russian Army would push on to their aid. Once the Poles were fully committed to the battle, the Soviet forces sat on their hands and watched placidly while the Germans destroyed the most effective nucleus of anti-Communist leadership and strength in all of Poland. This pause was a remarkably calloused example of long-term political objectives getting precedence over immediate military advantage.

As an example of irregular warfare the Warsaw fighting during the next six weeks is quite possibly unique. The remarkable discipline and staying power of the Polish Home Army and the expert use it made of the inadequate weapons it possessed, proved without question that it had evolved from a guerrilla resistance force into a first-class military unit. But determination and courage were not enough. The superior German forces reoccupied what was left of the city and destroyed its defenders.

For all these reasons, open revolt in cities and built-up areas has become more and more the prerogative of regular military forces, for they are the only ones which possess the weapons, equipment, and training to overcome the security and military forces of a large city and seize effective control. It was the Argentine Army that overthrew the national government and forced Perón to flee; and Nasser and Kassim, both of them professional officers, used their control of the military forces to bring them to power in Egypt and Iraq.

In this connection it is interesting to note that Castro has greatly reduced the influence of the regular Cuban Army since he came to power. Many of its officers have been purged, and every effort has been made to build up the power and position of the more lightly armed and loosely organized militia, most of whose members are reliably loyal to the regime. Castro and his fellow leaders are fully aware of the perils of a large-scale military revolt, which might take over Havana or the provincial cities, and are doing everything possible to reduce this danger to the minimum.

The urban rebel who cannot count on military assistance has to work with great care and discretion if he is to escape the overwhelming attention of the police and the military. Like his country cousin, the rural guerrilla, he has to compensate for his combat weakness by superior mobility, intelligence, and knowledge of the battlefield. These terms have a slightly different meaning in the urban situation than in the jungle and forest, but in essence they are the same. Similarly the government must seek to trap the rebel, force him into battle on unfavorable terms, and isolate him from the general population.

The side streets, the alleys, the rooftops, and the sewers are the jungle trails of the urban guerrilla. These are his refuges, his bases, and his concentration points. His mobility depends in part on his intimate knowledge of these places, and in this regard he may be in a stronger position than the rural guerrilla. In many ways, the mazes of the Algerian Casbah and the twisted alleys and shanty towns of great cities like Calcutta and Singapore are more difficult for the authorities to search completely than is the thickest jungle or the most rugged hill country. Equally important to the urban rebel is his understanding of the workings of the government he is trying to overthrow. The reactions and countermeasures which certain acts are likely to evoke from the authorities, the patterns which investigations or raids will follow, the attitudes which different officials will take toward different situations; it is a knowledge of these matters that will provide the rebel leader with the freedom and the time, both fruits of mobility, to carry on his work.

The city rebel has many potential sources of intelligence, for the enemy is bound to be observed in almost everything that he does, and he has few ways of knowing who, among the entire population, may be watching and reporting on him. The authorities cannot isolate the rebel from the population or prevent his access to the sources of supply and information which serve the public as a whole. The urban rebel is not, like Mao's famous description of the guerrilla, a fish swimming in the sea of the population. Rather he is a handful of something very like sea water himself and cannot be swept up by the most efficient fish net.

But if the discreet city rebel is relatively immune from military countermeasures, he is painfully vulnerable to detection and exposure by traitors and spies who manage to infiltrate his organization. The leader of urban insurgents must be even more careful and selective in recruiting his lieutenants and followers than is the guerrilla leader in the field. In the city he cannot exercise the same degree of control and discipline over them, and this unavoidable looseness of organization and the fact that the authorities are always near at hand means that the danger of betrayal is always high. Therefore, the leader, in most instances, tries to build the loyalty of his group on top of existing loyalties or bonds which already exist among them. The rebel who then wavers in his loyalty to the movement will hesitate to leave or betray it because of ties to relations, friends, or old associates who are also involved. The leader who can build his effort around members of social, religious, racial, or professional groups which already have some measure of cohesion is in a stronger position than one who must recruit from a heterogeneous population.

Concentration on special groups in a population is certainly not limited to urban insurrections only. Rebel movements of all sorts have found great strength by concentrating on homogeneous elements. Recent examples have been the Mau Mau insurrection in Kenya, which centered almost entirely in the Kikuiu tribe, and the EOKA rebellion in Cyprus, which was built from the more militant elements in the Greek sections of the population. Similarly, the OAS, the French movement that opposed any compromise with the nationalist forces in Algeria and sought to terrorize Paris and the cities of Algeria, was built around dissatisfied elements in the officer corps of the regular French Army.

Over a period of years the national Communist parties within the free world have sought to develop a strong cohesion within themselves. When they expand they look for their additional support among special groupings in the society, for where positive grievances and frustrated aspirations are creating tensions within a population these are usually most sharply focused in one element. Traditionally the Communists have sought to develop strength within labor unions on the theory that they will there find a general dissatisfaction with the existing order of things, and, particularly in the underdeveloped areas, there has been a corresponding emphasis placed on student associations. In part, this additional emphasis is placed on students because industrial labor has not yet become a political force in many of these states. Then, in many cases the level of education has outstripped the economic possibility of utilizing the sort of education provided, and the aroused expectations cannot be satisfied. In students, rebel leaders find individuals with a broad basis of common opinion and aspiration and a relatively narrow basis of experience on which to judge the wisdom and feasibility of given actions. As a general thing students have a readiness for rowdiness which, with training and guidance, can be built into a fine talent for rebellious violence. At the same time their desire to conform to the opinions and standards of their fellows exerts a strong disciplinary influence on them. The Communists have made excellent use of youth groups in a number of cities of the free world, their virtually complete control of the Chinese Middle Schools in Singapore being an example of this. Conversely, the evident emphasis that they place on the indoctrination and control of the youth in their own countries shows that they do not intend to let any alien influences sway their youngsters away from them.

Government authorities confronting an urban rebellion find that their constant proximity to their enemy can be both an advantage and a handicap. They are always in a position to act quickly on any information they receive, and there is none of the difficulty of reaching out to guerrilla bases in remote fastnesses. The city rebel may well be hidden a few yards down the street from police headquarters. The pressing problem in fighting the city insurgent is to make him show himself or to find

him among the crowds in the streets and rabbit warrens of a
great town.

In seeking to find and seize the rebel, the official is caught on
the horns of an almost unescapable dilemma; and here again his
difficulties are essentially political. The rebels' objective is to dis-
credit the government and to make it impossible for the authorities to govern. If officials wish to secure and hold popular
support, they must prevent the rebels from gaining these ends
and must demonstrate their own interest and concern for the
public welfare. Unfortunately for them, just about every step
which officials can take to isolate and cope with insurgents in a
city interrupts and hinders the normal processes of orderly life
and trade—the very things which the government is trying to
protect.

Curfews, travel limitations, check points for identity papers,
and spot searches of buildings and individuals may be necessary
steps for the authorities if they are to hold down rebel activity,
and essential if the government is to protect the population from
increasing coercion by the rebels, but these moves work against
the government in two serious ways.

First, they are public signals of the government's concern at
the activity and, by implication, at the strength of the rebel movement. As was suggested earlier, a resistance movement becomes
really serious at the moment when the people begin, as a whole,
to take it seriously. They are much more likely to do so when they
see evidence that the authorities themselves are concerned, and
such evidence is hard to conceal in a crowded area.

Second, control measures almost invariably irritate and alienate the people they are designed to defend. Even the most
enlightened and farsighted political program of reform and development is weakened or nullified if the people come to feel
that they are being hedged about with unwarranted limits on
their freedom of action. In this situation, the rebel propagandists
have the best of it coming and going. They can either take the

line that the restrictions are unnecessary, absurd, and merely another indication that the incompetent authorities should be replaced, or they can claim that the insurgent movement is far too strong to be slowed down by such petty hindrances, and that the restrictions are the last desperate twitchings of a regime that is nearly dead.

The government officials are placed in a difficult position in this sort of conflict. They must take strong action to counter the evident disorders, but in some measures, they weaken themselves by the very admission that such action is needed. Certainly they make their situation far more awkward if their corrective measures are clumsily or brutally carried out. Few things are more useful to a struggling rebellion than a few bona fide martyrs, and, if the government hopes to retain a broad base of popular support, it must see that its officers use the minimum open force necessary and apply it adroitly. Mass reprisals and the arrest and detention of innocent bystanders will rapidly alienate supporters of the government, and the true offenders are far harder to spot in an urban than in a rural setting. Anything approaching a witch hunt is bound to create a general feeling that the government does not have an effective plan for meeting its difficulties, that its leaders do not really understand the sources of their troubles, and that they have panicked. Under these circumstances, the popular feeling may very well be right.

This is not to say that the threat or the problems it creates can safely be underestimated or shoved under the rug, but if the authorities can project to the population an impression of efficiency and confidence in meeting any urban crisis, be it an epidemic, a bad fire, or a rebellion, they will have moved a long way toward controlling the situation.

Knowledgeable and prompt action by police and constabulary are just as important as operations by the military forces in coping with any insurrection or guerrilla rising. In coping with rebellion within cities the role of the police becomes infinitely more important. Most governments are aware of the psychological dangers that attend using soldiers to serve as substitutes or reinforcements for police and other security forces. Not only do the rebels gain considerable prestige from the fact that the government has to use its heaviest instrument of force against them, but armed soldiers represent an alien element in the average citizen's daily life, particularly in cities, and they are resented as such. As already mentioned, well-armed troops can be brutally effective in suppressing insurrection within the confines of a city, but even if the soldiers' behavior is exemplary and no lives are lost, the very fact that they are brought on the scene gives an appearance of cruelty and harshness which is meat for the rebels' propaganda.

This is particularly true in nations which have become accustomed to Anglo-Saxon concepts of maintaining law and order. When, in the summer of 1932, General MacArthur obeyed a presidential order to drive the Bonus Marchers off the encampment they had set up on the Anacostia flats outside of Washington and sent his troops in to do the job, the national reaction was one of revulsion both to the act itself and, somewhat unfairly, to the general who carried out the order. This reaction occurred despite the fact that the situation was clearly beyond the control of the local police. Some forty years earlier, during the depression year of 1894, another forlorn group, an unemployed collection known as Coxey's Army, had straggled to Washington planning to impress their demands on the government. On that occasion Coxey had been arrested by the police on the somewhat dubious charge of trespassing on the Capitol grounds, and his followers gradually drifted away. Both solutions seem pretty harsh, but there can be little question that the earlier one caused less resentment and left fewer political wounds.

In deciding whether or not to use troops to suppress urban rebellion and violence the government must also consider the effect that the move will have on the troops themselves. If the authorities lose the loyalty and support of their own military forces during a period of revolt, they are in really serious trouble. Troops will rarely have qualms about fighting and killing armed guerrillas when they are often suffering a disproportionate number of casualties themselves. It is quite another thing to ask troops to use lethal force on youths of their own nationality who are throwing stones.

Probably the most effective instrument that a government can bring to bear against a campaign of urban violence is an efficient police intelligence service or, to use the less palatable term for it, a good secret police. If the leaders, the plans, and the methods of the rebellious movement are known to the authorities, the likelihood of its being able to mount major demonstrations or to strike serious blows is sharply reduced and, like a guerrilla force cut off from its bases, the movement has to fall back on the defensive. Of course, the government of a state that works on democratic principles must be discreet and temperate in handling a secret police force. Like the introduction of troops, the use of clandestine methods of investigation and entrapment strikes a chord of opposition in most peoples that runs very deep. This reaction is commendable, but no one can conceive of a modern government controlling crime and subversion without some sort of secret police. Americans have solved this dilemma by exalting the F.B.I. as the protector of democratic concepts and by seeing to it that the quality of its personnel assures that this exaltation is in large measure justified. The British also have always ensured that the quality of their secret security services is sufficiently high to allay any reasonable fears as to their proper functioning. Through many parts of the world the concept of a secret police has been accepted more resignedly as a proper function of government, and the political liabilities inherent in its relatively open use are correspondingly diminished. Nevertheless arbitrary or abusive use of the police power will always produce intense public resentment, and a government with any democratic aspirations is bound to be damaged in the long run by actions that smack of authoritarianism.

Governmental planning on effective political countermeasures for urban uprisings is complicated by the variances in the quality of the leadership in such rebellions and the rationality of the goals the leaders are seeking. At times it is hard to tell exactly what the insurgents are fighting for.

This is not the case, of course, when the rebels in a city are receiving their orders and guidance from the leaders of a national movement which has a definite program for the overthrow of the existing government and its replacement with another system. Such leaders are aware of the growing importance of the swelling urban populations of the underdeveloped areas and realize that if they are to achieve national power they must gain control over these newly important peoples through whom they have their best chance of striking at the centers of government power. A rebellious movement in a city, as in the countryside, must identify itself with some popular cause and at least appear to be working in the interest of reforms or concessions which appeal to a substantial part of the population. The rebel leaders must make the same decisions on the balance of the "stick and carrot"—the same balance of honest conversion versus terrorism that confronts the leaders of guerrilla bands. They must work out the advantages of coercive terrorism toward the noncooperative elements in the population and of violent attacks on the authorities with the losses of sympathy and voluntary support that are certain to accompany these actions.

The urban rebel leader, utilizing cohesive groups of supporters and holding advantages both in intelligence procurement and in the rather specialized form of mobility mentioned earlier, can seek a number of tactical objectives. Assuming that his ultimate goal is to overthrow the government, his approach will depend on his estimate of his own strength relative to that of the government. Since he must always seek to increase the strength and number of his own following, he must limit the amount of disruptive action directly attributable to him, for he cannot afford to have public sentiment swing against him unless he is able and willing to secure his needed public support entirely through the use of terror.

As with the leader of rural guerrillas, his usual aim is to cause the government as much inconvenience and trouble as he can. To this end he can operate in the political and economic, although not the straight military, fields.

Strikes, ranging from minor tie-ups in one factory to general stoppages which may paralyze much of a city, are direct and commonly used economic weapons. These disturbances can be brought to the desired level of violence by introducing outside sympathizers and demonstrators whose task it is to work up a riot. For example, in Singapore and other Oriental cities the Communists have worked this one-two combination on a number of occasions by bringing student groups to demonstrate at the scene of a strike. The alleged repression of the demonstration is then made the basis of new strikes, and the process can be repeated so long as the leaders feel that there is profit in the game.

The fact that rebels in a city have little chance of taking over full political control in the face of superior government, military, and police power does not in any way mean that these operations are not highly profitable. If the government is already in serious trouble, disturbances of this sort will hasten its decline. If the main emphasis and major opportunity for a rebellion lies in operations in the woods and forests, city-bred trouble will prevent the authorities from concentrating their full power against the country guerrillas.

Sometimes the very existence of the simmering revolt will trigger outside pressures and events which in themselves will bring about the results that the rebels are striving for. An instance of this was the course of the EOKA resistance movement among the Greek element of the population of Cyprus. Never, through their own efforts alone, could those insurgents have forced the withdrawal of British authority from the island, but for a time they occupied the undivided attention of a large body of British troops and police and managed to attract well-nigh worldwide attention to their effort. By managing to keep the rebellion alive they managed to elevate the issue over which they were fighting to a level where it directly involved the foreign relations of three nations—Britain, Greece, and Turkey—threatened the effectiveness and unity of the southern flank of NATO, and weakened Britain's whole position in the Middle East. The end result was that the movement caused trouble and dissension on a scale wholly out of proportion to its limited physical assets and finally achieved independence for Cyprus.

The OAS, the French secret army organization which tried to prevent any negotiated peace between the French Government and the FLN in Algeria, was another resistance movement, essentially urban, which strove for political objectives far more ambitious than its physical strength and political following could justify. By indiscriminate attacks on Arab civilians, the OAS leadership evidently believed it could so exacerbate French-Algerian relations that the Algerians would be provoked into massive countermeasures, that full-scale war would be resumed, and that no settlement would be possible. By selective bombings and attacks on prominent French public figures who opposed the organization's policies, they apparently believed they could terrorize these men into opposing the Government's policy of seeking a cease-fire and settlement. Their ultimate hope was to leave the French Government with no alternative but to prolong and finally to win the Algerian war, but the leaders of the movement were significantly silent as to how they expected this victory to be achieved or what they expected it to look like, once achieved.

From a political angle the OAS deserves some careful consideration. It was a rebellion dedicated to political objectives which were only vaguely defined, but had a high emotional charge. On its own the movement could not possibly restore effective French authority in Algeria. Instead it had to depend on the influence it could exert on the major parties involved. There are no visible indicators that the organization tried to convert individuals and groups outside the Army to its cause, but rather took the wholly negative line of obstructionism and terror. If, indeed, its leaders could have brought about major defections from the French military forces it would have established the conditions in which a true *coup d'état* can take place, but the chances of this grew slimmer and slimmer as time passed.

Here, then, was a political rebellion essentially urban in origin and operation, with no realizable aims and not much of a base from which to work. Its military affiliations enabled its members to procure the plastic explosives and weapons with which they could make a nuisance of themselves, but there was no forward momentum to the effort as a whole.

Paradoxically this very aimlessness, this negative obstructionism, created special problems for the government in dealing with the movement. Since the force of the rebellion was emotional and not rational, no program of reasonable reform and development could erode away the fanatical foundation on which it was built. The members of such a group do not consider themselves criminals, but the anti-social nature of their effort leaves the government little choice but to treat them as such.

The more violent anarchists of the middle and late nineteenth century presented the government of the Latin nations of Europe with somewhat similar problems. These men did not seek reforms and improvements in government; rather they conceived that all government was bad and should be done away with. A position like this leaves even the most enlightened authorities very little to get hold of, and it effectively forces them to suppress totally the adamant rebels who will accept no viable solution to the country's problems.

As the underdeveloped nations move forward to modernize and industrialize their societies, we are bound to see an increase in unrest and rebellion by groups which are dissatisfied with their conditions and what they see going on about them, but have no firm idea what they can do to improve things. To people caught in this emotional vise, violence for its own sake comes to look increasingly attractive, if only to demonstrate to themselves that they have some apparent control over the forces they feel are penning them in.

This problem and this reaction are not limited to the underdeveloped nations. Interesting and distressing signs of it show up in virtually every dynamic society when minority elements seek dramatic ways to demonstrate their dissatisfaction and assert their individuality. In this country during the early nineteen sixties we have seen indignant middle-aged businessmen, virtually all city dwellers, grasping rifles and crawling about the wood lots of the Middle and Far West, practicing at playing guerrillas. While some of these would-be warriors may have sincerely expected the arrival of the Russians, most of them were showing mild and silly symptoms of the same malady.

Far more serious is the situation to be found in the schools of many of the nation's cities. Anyone wishing to explore the problems of non-directional urban rebellion would do well to look at the difficulties faced by the New York City Board of Education every day of the school year. This is no place to examine the dilemmas of juvenile delinquency and gang wars, but it is worth bearing in mind some of the parallels between this social blight which is troubling us at home and the adult disorders and insurrections which are threatening the less stable nations of the free world.

American youngsters in the slums of our cities are making and using homemade pistols or zip guns which are just as effective as many of those produced in the guerrilla arsenals of South Vietnam. The tactics used by juvenile gangs in their feuds and in evading the authorities are essentially the same as those of older political rebels. Superior mobility, intelligence, and knowledge of the ground is equally important to both. For different reasons both groups are dissatisfied with life as they are leading it or as they see it shaping up for them. Neither group has the strength to overcome the authorities, but both have the capacity to cause grave inconvenience and dislocation to the immediate society in which they live.

Luckily for us, the social and economic reforms and improvements which will ease the inchoate drives and compulsions that produce most juvenile delinquency are within our capabilities, and in many areas the situation is already improving. However, the pressures and tensions that make for political unrest and violence in the growing urban areas of the free world are most certainly not being solved satisfactorily in many places, and over the coming decades the problem is likely to grow more acute. We and the nations directly threatened will have to find ways of handling these difficulties and easing the shocks of industrialization, or we are going to face serious political, economic, and, ultimately, military setbacks.

V

Sabotage and Espionage

Many generations ago, the French peasants and early industrial workers discovered the value of their sabots, or wooden shoes, as destructive weapons. During strikes or layoffs, a sabot thrown into machinery or simply stamped up and down on anything breakable produced a satisfying amount of damage. Thus the word sabotage came into being.

Sabotage, or the clandestine destruction of property, is an integral part of unconventional and irregular war. The military weakness of guerrillas and rebels which forces them to avoid battle with official forces except through ambushes, assassinations, and hit-and-run raiding, also frequently limits them to more or less covert attacks on the government's material strength.

Almost certainly the first American venture in this field took place in Boston Harbor, when young men, painted as Indians, rather lightheartedly clambered aboard three merchant vessels and threw overboard their cargoes of tea in protest against the tax levied on it. However, our concept of sabotage has changed a good deal since the night of the notable Tea Party. In 1916 occurred the famous Black Tom explosion, in which a large stock of munitions, stored on a pier near Jersey City, blew up with a blast that rocked the New York area and caused twenty-two million dollars worth of damage. Although it was not until 1939 that a Mixed Claims Commission finally found Germany guilty of causing the explosion, this had been immediately and widely assumed to be the case, and there has since been a tendency to equate sabotage with sinister forms of espionage. As we shall see later this is not usually the case.

Luckily for urban populations, incidents like the Black Tom explosion are extremely rare, but spectacular catastrophes, occurring during periods of war or serious tension, are always suspected of being sabotage, even when the cause is honest human error or an evident act of God. In 1942 the great French liner SS *Normandie,* renamed the U.S.S. *Lafayette,* was lying at dockside in New York being converted for duty as a troopship when a fire broke out, spread rapidly, and got out of control. The ship finally capsized where she lay under the weight of water poured into her in an effort to put out the fires. Afterwards, a congressional subcommittee examined the circumstances in great detail and concluded that the fire had been an accident —that there had been culpable carelessness, but that no evidence of sabotage existed. Still for years it was the almost universal belief of the public that the great ship had been done in by an evil German spy.

When a saboteur is able to wreak destruction on as cataclysmic a scale as this, it is almost always because the local guard system or the security system of the government as a whole is woefully weak. Of course, an ammunition dump or an immobilized ship, unmanned and filled with scaffolding and paint, is the stuff that saboteurs' dreams are made of, but the task of attacking most important targets is considerably harder than peaceful laymen realize. Here again, movies and popular literature have created some odd impressions. Heroes or villains destroy in a few moments, with charges they can carry on their backs, steel bridges that in actuality could only be brought down after extensive work by trained engineers using a small truckload of explosives.

In theory, a single well-planned act of sabotage could damage a whole economy. If it were possible to select the most important

element in a given industry, choose the most important factory or
link in this element, find the most crucial machine therein and
finally destroy its most important part, the entire structure should
at least falter. But as is so often the case, theory and practice
are far apart.

There are some targets that stand out so obviously as fruitful
targets for sabotage that any rebel can recognize them, and no
amount of government secrecy or deception can disguise their
significance. In this country, for instance, serious damage to the
"Soo" Locks on the Great Lakes would have painful and early
results, and anyone driving in or out from Washington National
Airport can visualize the complications that would follow a major
injury to the single railroad bridge over the Potomac. But it is
precisely because of their obvious importance that targets of this
sort are so carefully guarded in times of war.

Less obvious, but still important targets may be more easily
reached by the insurgent saboteur, but they are often hard for
him to identify. Air Force planning staffs assign some of their
best minds to the complicated and demanding task of selecting
targets for bombing since the costs of misdirected effort are obvious and appallingly high. Factors considered in selection include the importance of any potential target in the economic
or military structure of the enemy, its military vulnerability,
and the losses that an attack upon it would probably entail. For
the saboteur working with a guerrilla band or an insurgent group
within a city, calculations of this kind are just about impossible,
for the detailed and timely intelligence on which they must be
based is rarely available and, in most instances, he does not have
the military and economic training necessary to arrive at a reliably sound decision. Then too, attacks on special and highly
guarded sabotage targets almost always require meticulous tactical planning and execution, and the fragile nature of irregular
forces always leaves the insurgent leader uncertain whether or
not his semi-trained men may fail him at a critical moment.

Lawrence and his Arabs were given only one crucial target to destroy at a specific time during their campaign in World War I. That was the Yarmak Gorge railroad bridge, over which all Turkish reinforcements would have to pass once the British forces began their final offensive north into Palestine. The Arab attack was well planned, but the guerrillas carrying the explosives needed for the job broke and ran when they encountered relatively light opposition from the Turkish guards on the bridge, and the effort was a failure. Significantly, when the British authorities in World War II realized the imperative necessity of sabotaging or destroying the German facilities which were producing small quantities of heavy water in Norway, they did not count on the small but enthusiastic Norwegian resistance forces to carry out the mission. A small team of specially-trained and -equipped men was sent in to do the job.

In fact, effective sabotage campaigns by guerrillas and rebels depend for most of their impact on the cumulative results of many small acts by a large number of people. The rubber tree that is tapped a little too deeply and thus killed, the electrical circuit that is "accidentally" overloaded, the vehicle or machine that is improperly lubricated, and the freight consignment that is hopelessly misdirected—these are the things which can cause real injury if they occur frequently enough. Destructive clumsiness and carelessness, quite literally woodenshoeing, is a far harder thing for a government to cope with than the activity of a single villain in a black cloak.

There is no question that more precisely directed attacks can cause more physical damage, but the lack of focus provides some compensating advantages. This is the same rough balance of advantages found in the conduct of some purely military operations. For example, the rarely attained ideal in dropping paratroop units is to get the men with their equipment down in a compact drop zone from which they can move into action rapidly as an organized and relatively complete military unit. Given the vagaries of low-level aerial navigation, wind, and the obvious difficulties of men finding each other in strange country in the dark, this is hardly ever achieved. Most combat drops spread men and gear over a large area. The isolated small groups can be fairly effective as combat units, but it is usually some time before the whole force is brought under one cohesive command.

This initial dispersion and the confusion that inevitably accompanies it are certainly weaknesses, but they present the defending enemy with some problems and decisions they would be spared in fighting a united force. The defender cannot quickly determine the location of the main attacking threat, the objective of the attack, or the strength of the attacking force. At the time when he can least afford delay, he often cannot find a target at which to strike.

An exaggerated instance of this took place during the Allied landings at Salerno, Italy during World War II, when an American airborne battalion was to be dropped some twenty miles inland near the village of Avellino to block the roads in that immediate area. In the event, very few planes located their drop zones and the men were scattered over more than a hundred square miles of Italian countryside. Nevertheless, fighting alone or in small groups, the paratroopers mined roads, ambushed small enemy units, blew bridges and, while losing a fifth of their number, managed to raise a commendable amount of hell. In evaluating the pros and cons of the operation, General James Gavin wrote that "It disrupted German communications and partly blocked their supplies and reserves. It also caused the enemy to keep units on antiparachute missions that otherwise could have been used at the point of his main effort at Salerno. In fact, he used many more troops for corrective and preventive purposes against the airborne troops than were committed by the Allied high command."[1]

[1] Major General James M. Gavin, "Airborne Warfare," *Infantry Journal Press*, Washington, 1947, p. 32.

In combating widespread simple sabotage it is an endless task to pin down the responsibility for multitudinous little failures and errors, and once again it becomes evident that the only true solution to a government's problem in coping with popular unrest lies in the political field. Tight security measures will certainly reduce the amount of sabotage carried out, but so long as people wish to strike at the government, acts of sabotage will be attempted and some will be successful.

Widespread sabotage inevitably indicates that widespread support for the rebel movement really exists, as individual acts of minor sabotage cannot be enforced by even the best-disciplined and most ruthlessly terroristic cadres and leaders. When fourteen thousand trees are cut down in a single night, as happened on French farms in Algeria in 1956, the loss of the trees may disturb the authorities deeply, but far more disturbing is the proof positive that a large proportion of the population must have willingly participated in the act.

Since widespread acts of minor sabotage, unlike the provision of supplies and information to guerrilla bands, reflect more accurately the convictions of the people than the ability of the rebels to coerce them into action, the number of such incidents is a pretty fair indicator of the popularity and standing of the government with the citizenry. When the sympathies of the people no longer lead them to favor the rebels, widely scattered acts of simple sabotage will begin to drop off, even though terror and fear of reprisals may still protect the identity of the rebel leaders and assure them of needed support for other types of operations.

Even if their popular support declines, the active insurgents will continue to attack and sabotage the communications and transportations systems and those industrial targets that they can reach. The attacks of these active rebels may be more expertly carried out, and the targets selected may be more significant and important. Still, the task of the government security forces is likely to grow substantially simpler. A pattern begins to emerge in the attacks, making it easier to protect likely targets, and the field of likely suspects is greatly narrowed. It is the random quality of popularly conducted sabotage that makes it so difficult to prevent.

The American tendency to link sabotage with espionage springs in part from the nature and composition of the Communist Party in the United States. As we have already seen, in regions where a movement such as a national Communist party has little or no foundation of popular support and poor prospects of gaining any, it has to limit itself to activities which can be carried on by a relatively small number of dedicated members among a generally unfriendly population. Revolutionary groups attempting to work in the United States are in this position. Their members enjoy the legal protections accorded to all citizens, and they don't have to worry that their actions will lose them any popular support, for they have virtually none to lose. Under these circumstances, the members of the group, aware that they cannot overthrow the government themselves, undertake to serve as best they can a foreign power that may be able to do so. Espionage, and to a lesser extent, sabotage then become their natural, and just about their only, weapons.

Both we and the British have had some unpleasant shocks since the war, as evidences of Communist espionage have come to light. The result has been a healthy series of improvements in the security systems and a considerably less healthy spell of spy hysteria in American political life. The fact is that during a period of fantastically rapid scientific development in both the free and the Communist worlds, the loss of temporarily valuable technical and other information has cost us only a fraction of what more open Communist operations have cost other lands. Communist concentration on espionage is in many ways an admission that more directly profitable courses of political action and attack are closed to them. Still, since this has been our own national problem, we sometimes tend to look for it in difficulties elsewhere, even when our own experiences, painful though they were, have relatively little direct application.

This is not to say that all insurrectionists, Communist and otherwise, do not set up the most efficient intelligence nets they can. As we have already seen, the survival and success of any rebellion depends directly on the quality of the information its leaders obtain. But most of the information needed and gathered by active rebels is for their own use in their own operations, rather than for the primary use of a foreign power which may be supporting and encouraging them. It is tactical rather than strategic stuff they are after, and procurement of "national secrets" of the sort traditionally associated with major espionage is only incidental to the direct advancement of the rebellion.

For these reasons, guerrillas usually make relatively little use of secret agents at the higher levels of government. Rebel leaders may be in hiding with a substantial price on their heads, but they are usually well known to the people by name, and often by appearance. If they gain successes, the effects of their work and their connection with it are evident to all—a situation that a really clandestine agent would find both embarrassing and dangerous.

Couriers who maintain communications between guerrilla groups and the rebel representatives who live among the people and arrange for the supplies, recruits, and information reaching the active rebels obviously must avoid the attentions of the authorities, and hence seek a degree of anonymity, but in most cases these people are well known in their own localities, and they are protected either by a general sympathy for the work they are doing or by a well-justified fear of the fate of known informers.

Thus, while an insurrection depends for its success on avoiding unwelcome contact with the police and military forces, there is probably less emphasis on espionage and high-level spies in this sort of conflict than there is in a conventional international war.

VI

Military Technology and the Guerrilla

Rivers of ink have been poured out during the past few years describing the changing nature of modern warfare. Much of the flow has been devoted to nuclear energy in both weapons and propulsion systems, missiles, and the possible future military uses of space. All of these areas of conflict involve awesomely complicated technology and, perhaps, as a reaction to the complexity and sophistication of the weapons required in other forms of modern war, there has been a tendency to think of unconventional and guerrilla warfare as a return to entirely elemental conflict, without benefit of modern refinements and technology. There is no question that guerrilla war has been altered less obviously than have other forms of fighting, and the knife and the bamboo spear retain a military importance that they long ago lost elsewhere. Nevertheless, new developments play a major role in these struggles, presenting many new opportunities and problems both to the authorities and to the rebels.

For our purposes, the changes can best be considered in terms of transportation, communications, and weaponry. These changes must be weighed against that tactical mobility, intelligence, and superior knowledge of the terrain which, together with appropriate striking power, we have already seen to be the essentials of any successful insurrection.

The effect of roads and railroads on the conduct of guerrilla warfare has already been touched on. The better the road net of a nation, the more difficult it is for guerrillas to operate effectively, for the authorities are better able to deploy their forces to and within the disturbed areas. This is all net gain for the military forces so long as they are tactically able to take the highways or leave them alone. Their great danger, as we have seen, is that they will develop a sort of logistic alcoholism which leaves them weak and jittery when deprived of the highroads.

If this military disease takes hold, the guerrillas are doubly strengthened. They are more secure than ever in their remote bases, and they are assured of suitable and, frequently, highly vulnerable targets for ambush. There is no known way by which a truck convoy on a country road, particularly in thick country, can be wholly protected from the threat of ambush if the government does not have effective control of the country on both sides of the road. Armored cars can protect the personnel riding in them from roadside small arms fire, but they can be disabled and halted by mines, after which they become a steel trap for the men in them. Of course, most military vehicles are not armored, and the threat to the soldiers in them naturally increases.

But often the surprised soldiers in ambushed convoys can inflict heavier casualties on guerrilla attackers than the latter can stand on a repeated and long-sustained basis. The vast majority of felled trees and other road blocks which hamper and delay military movements in guerrilla-infested areas are found to be unmanned and undefended. Still, each barrier takes its toll on the nerves of the troops. The routine fanning out and checking of the road ahead is tiring and frustrating when nothing is found. Then there is the ever-present possibility of a crash of fire from the undergrowth, the dive for cover, knowing that the roadside ditch may well be mined or sown with sharpened stakes, the desperate effort to counterattack at what is often only the flash of enemy weapons, and the sickening certainty that one's own losses are almost certain to be far greater than those of the scarcely seen foe.

Ambush fighting can be costly to both sides, in material and men, but it is crucially important for the government to keep the major roads open. They can provide the precious additional measure of mobility which its troops must have to defeat the guerrillas. Equally important, the partially protected highways bind the country together as nothing else can, for they can reduce and finally destroy the sense of isolation in the regions far from the capital and the major cities which gives the revolt its best chance to flourish.

All guerrilla leaders have realized the threat that improved roads and highways pose for them. This has been shown again and again in their constant efforts, not only to destroy the military traffic traveling on them, but to destroy the bridges and the roads themselves whenever they are able to do so.

Railroads present guerrillas with essentially the same threats and opportunities as do highways. The tonnage carried by trains is almost always much greater than that moved by road convoys, and for most underdeveloped nations in the early stages of modernization and industrialization the railroads are usually more important to the economy than are the truck roads and highways. Railroad traffic is generally more vulnerable to guerrilla attack than that of the roads, for the weight and rigidity of railroad rolling stock makes almost any wreck a highly destructive affair. A train, with all the freight it is carrying, can hardly be written off as can a few trucks. Trained crews with special equipment, including cranes and heavy jacks, are usually needed to get the line clear again, and the delay is bound to be considerable. For a guerrilla, the military equivalent of a ten-strike is to wreck a train in a tunnel where no crane can be brought in, the wreckage cannot be rolled off the line, the tunnel itself may be damaged, and the tie-up is certain to be a long one.

Damaging railroads to any significant extent does take either a good deal of time and labor or an adequate supply of explosives. However, when demolition supplies are available, track is a far juicier target than all but the most important highways. Roads can be used even when they are in pretty bad shape. This is being demonstrated in South Vietnam today, where a common Viet Cong practice is to dig large numbers of closely set pits in important highways, leaving only a narrow path along one side. In turn the authorities try to see to it that these holes are filled in, and frequently they call in for labor the very villagers who were dragooned into digging the same holes the night before. As a result, the roads so treated become pretty sketchy at the best of times and downright alarming in the rainy seasons, but they still serve their purpose.

Railroads are far less elastic. Either they work moderately well or they break down completely. Repairing blown-out roadbeds is laborious and time-consuming. Burned ties, or blasted metal ones where they are used, and twisted or broken rails present serious problems, particularly in regions where these items are hard to come by. Restoring the track to service requires an effort and expenditure that is wholly out of proportion to that of the guerrillas in doing the damage.

In addition to all this, attacks on rail lines produce a frequently valuable by-product for insurgents. Efficient management of a single- or even double-tracked line calls for careful planning and scheduling at all times, and the difficulties become far greater if faulty maintenance or enemy attacks have left the system short of engines. As a result of rebel attacks, schedules may be thrown out, engines may be destroyed, shipments may be lost or misdirected in the confusion. Consequently, marshaling yards and sidings begin to fill up with cars waiting to be sorted out and moved. As the number of these immobilized targets increases they become the natural prey of saboteurs, for they become more and more difficult to guard. Thus the government's problems compound themselves.

It is worth noting that the dangers to the government of stalled and snarled-up rail traffic become particularly serious when the rebels are operating in support of a foreign enemy in a time of open war. Congested railroad marshaling yards can make very rewarding targets for accurate air attack.

Insurgent attacks on modern transportation facilities, like so many other moves in unconventional warfare, have political consequences for both the rebels and the authorities, and these must be carefully considered by both. Where the highway or railroad is being used for purely military purposes these factors are not important, but this situation is relatively rare, and in most cases these facilities are highly important to the economic and social life of the people. Their destruction is directly and often deeply felt and, since the injury is clearly the result of rebel action, the insurgents risk alienating popular sympathy if the damage is excessive. The Viet Cong technique of damaging roads, which was mentioned above, shows that they are aware of this danger. The trenches dug prevent the passage of military vehicles, while the narrow path that is usually left allows bicycles and foot traffic to continue unhampered.

If the rebels can be sure of wholehearted and self-sacrificing backing, this risk is not so serious, and when guerrilla leaders are depending almost entirely on coercion and terrorism to obtain their popular support they are likely to disregard it entirely. Then they can assume that any damage inflicted will simply add to the military and economic difficulties of the authorities and will, therefore, work to the rebels' advantage.

The government, on the other hand, can make propaganda use of wanton destruction by the insurgents, but this line must be handled with care. Every denunciation of the rebels' calloused disregard of the public welfare is at the same time an admission of the authorities' evident inability to protect the interests of the people and their weakness in the face of open attack.

The full impact of modern instantaneous communications on irregular warfare lagged far behind that of modern transportation, for the telegraph proved woefully vulnerable to guerrilla attack in contested areas. During the last hundred years this was demonstrated repeatedly by the American Indians, by the French *franc-tireurs* who fought on against the Prussians after the French defeats of 1870, by the Boers, and by the Philippino insurrectionists. In these campaigns the regular military soon tired of setting up poles and lines for the guerrillas to cut down, so that heliograph and other light systems tended to replace telegraph in enemy infested regions.

Telephone lines are obviously just as vulnerable to guerrilla sabotage and attack. Furthermore, the premium that guerrilla operations place on speed and lightness of equipment makes the laying of wires for command phones in tactical situations far less useful and more costly than in slower-moving conventional fights. In his book on guerrilla war in Cuba, Che Guevara made the interesting statement that the Castro forces set up an extensive phone system and found it useful for linking widely separated elements. This certainly confirms his assertion that the bases the guerrillas established in the thickly wooded mountains were completely secure from attack, and indicates that the government's patrol activity in the country between these bases was very limited indeed. Even so, the guerrillas' use of a phone system is a little surprising. The danger of the authorities stumbling on one of the lines and either following it to its ends or tapping it as an intelligence source would seem to outweigh any possible advantage that the phones could have provided for the rebels.

It was the advent of radio that revolutionized the communications used in unconventional war, and direct wireless communications is now taken for granted between tactical units in the field, between outposts and higher headquarters, and for coordination of air and ground operations. Since insurgents in the field are hardly well equipped for extensive radio monitoring, or code-breaking, they have relatively little chance of intercepting government messages, and even those tactical voice messages they may pick up and understand can do them relatively little good, except in those rare cases where the overheard word may give them sufficient notice to escape from a rapidly closing trap.

Possession of radio sets and transmitters is certainly helpful to guerrillas, but even the most rugged sets are subject to wear and breakage in the hard conditions of guerrilla life, and spare parts are hard to find and usually impossible to make. Hence, no widespread guerrilla movement can depend entirely on radio for links among its several parts.

When the guerrilla can count on supply and support from outside of the country where the battle is taking place, radio becomes more important for him. He has a chance to call for resupply and perhaps reinforcement. Using a station in the neighboring supporting country as an amplifying relay, he can communicate with other elements of the rebel movement which his own set may not be strong enough to reach, and he can receive up-to-date intelligence which may help him either to mount effective strikes or to save his skin from enemy surprises.

Despite these advantages gained, the use of radio is a potential danger to any guerrilla. His enemies, the government authorities, are in a good position to monitor and intercept his messages. They may be able to break and read these if they are in cypher, but even if they do not, they are very likely to get a directional fix on the point from which the message was sent. If two or more government monitoring stations hear his message the guerrilla's position can be determined by the authorities by triangulation and, if forces are available, they can close in on the indicated spot. Some of the modern methods of accelerated automatic transmission of messages can reduce the chance of enemy interception, but the chance still exists. The rebel radio operator and any other insurgents with him stand in real danger of being located and tracked down.

Then too, the guerrilla using radio stands the very serious danger of having one of the other sets and operators of the rebel movement captured and used against him. If the authorities can seize an operator with his radio and are able to talk or coerce him into cooperating with them, they can gain invaluable information on the whereabouts and activities of the guerrillas, and even to some extent control their operations until the rebels learn of the capture. This form of penetration can be particularly serious when the rebels are using radio extensively to communicate with friendly supporters outside of the country. During World War II the German counterintelligence got this sort of toe hold on some elements of the Dutch resistance. From intelligence gained through their secret control of a resistance radio the Germans were able to trace many of the Dutch leaders, and some Allied agents who were parachuted into the country found the Gestapo waiting for them as they landed. The resulting losses were high, and it took many months for the Allies and the remaining parts of the Dutch movement to determine what was happening to them and to reorganize on a secure basis.

In public communications the government enjoys a very considerable advantage over almost any insurgent opposition.

Radio broadcasting has become almost the primary means of government-to-people communications in many of the less-developed areas. Simple radio receiving sets are widely distributed, and in the absence of other prompt or reliable news media, word received over the radio takes on something of the authority of Holy Writ. Seizure of the main broadcasting station is a high-priority objective for the rebels in any attempt at revolution by *coup d'état*, for control of the recognized government radio transmitter is just as important in an insurrection as is control of the microphone in a rowdy political meeting.

Maintaining a reliable broadcasting system is obviously far easier for an established government than for an insurgent force. Even when the rebels are able to find and utilize the complex equipment needed for this work and can either generate or tap into the substantial amounts of power required, they still have to operate on a fly-by-night basis. Rudimentary direction-finding gear will give the government a very fair idea of the spot where the rebels are working and allow forces to concentrate against them. Frequent moves may permit the rebel station to stay in business for some time; indeed, at the time of writing, the Viet Cong have had a reasonably powerful broadcasting station working from constantly shifting bases not far from Saigon for a number of months. Still, any regularity of transmitting times over rebel stations is just about impossible. Shifts in transmitting frequencies to prevent detection and localization by the government are far more likely to confuse and lose potential listeners than to confound official monitors. The rebel broadcasts are therefore vulnerable to intense jamming whenever the government feels that they are enough of a nuisance to warrant the effort. The only defense that the rebels have against this is to transmit on a frequency so near to that of one of the government channels that jamming will interfere with both of them. However, this calls for a skilled operation and a competitively strong transmitting power, or the encroaching rebel signal will simply be swallowed up in the noise of the government message.

Effective broadcasting support for a rebel movement can best be provided by the foreign friends and supporters of the revolt. Radio Moscow and Radio Peiping both saturate Africa and the Near and Far Easts with local-language broadcasts, and it is these stations which provide the great bulk of the radio propaganda that supports the Communist insurrections in the underdeveloped regions.

The printed word in the press, pamphlets, and posters is much used for public communications during insurrections in areas where a sufficient percentage of the population is literate to warrant appeals. Here again the government holds a great advantage in influencing the political opinions and actions of the people. Rebel leaders always seek to get their views circulated, but even the lightest printing press is unwieldy, heavy, and often noisy.

Paper is not always easy to come by, and clandestine distribution on a meaningful scale is dangerous and difficult to organize. For all these reasons the authorities have most of the cards in this game, and it is their own fault if they do not play them well.

Often the rebels' most effective public communications are more symbolic than informative. A simple slogan which is widely and constantly repeated can have great political impact, for it demonstrates the breadth and pervasiveness of the movement. Probably the most celebrated of these symbols was the V for Victory sign used by the Allies in the Second World War. The . . . — symbol was scrawled on walls all over German-occupied Europe, and it reappeared as soon as the authorities scrubbed or painted it out.

The rebels' capabilities are naturally increased when they have outside support and supply, for then pamphlets, posters, and other propaganda material can be prepared in safety and sent in to the scene of the struggle; but the government retains its advantage in this field, for such items usually have a lower priority than combat or medical supplies.

Aviation, and the development of air power, has certainly affected the course and conduct of unconventional war more than any other technological development of the past generation. In general, air operations have strengthened the hand of the government in handling rebellions, and in some areas it has provided a decisive superiority. It became clear a long time ago that insurgents or guerrillas could not long survive in regions where they were subject to attack from the air and where the terrain provided little or no shelter from such attack. During the First World War, T. E. Lawrence was slightly wounded and a number of the Arab insurgents killed by what appeared to have been almost casual raids by light Turkish aircraft. Shortly after that war, the British faced a considerable problem in restoring order to the desert area which now makes up a good part of the state of Iraq. A combination of air observation and attack by the RAF and

ground operation by light and fast armored cars did the job, and
the campaign provides one of the few instances where irregular
forces were checked and subdued in their own territory by a
smaller number of regular military. During the following decade
the RAF demonstrated that unruly tribesmen on the northwest
frontier of what is now Pakistan could be kept in check by air
operation which damaged or merely scattered the herds of sheep
on which these tribes depended for their support. When such
operations were backed up by even limited offensive or punitive
operations by ground forces, open rebellion became an unprofitable activity. It seems safe to say that large-scale insurrections
will no longer be seen in desert areas where the government
holds undisputed and effective control of the air.

In cases where rebels have the backing and support of a
friendly outside power, supply by air has greatly strengthened
their position. A single sortie by a World War II bomber could
drop arms and an adequate initial ammunition supply for one
hundred men as well as a fair supply of boots, clothing, blankets,
and rudimentary medical equipment. During the 1961 fighting
in Laos, American newspapers carried pictures of Soviet cargo
aircraft dropping supplies to the Communist forces in that country, and over a period of time support of this sort can have a tremendous impact. The government's own air facilities provide
the rebels with highly rewarding targets. There are few things
more impervious to sabotage with light equipment than the
heavy concrete of a runway, but the fuel stores, the bomb dumps,
and the parked airplanes themselves are highly vulnerable.
These must be guarded, as must any static position, and the
troops committed to this duty detract from the total the government can use offensively against the guerrillas on the ground.

The government also faces some real limitations on the effective use of air power against irregulars. In forest or jungle areas
there is little or no chance of seeing much of what is happening
on the ground through the blanket of vegetation. Recently there

have been efforts to pierce this cover in forest areas by having airplanes spray out defoliants—chemicals which will poison and kill the leaves. Such sprays are used commercially along the rights of way of railroads and power lines in America, but their real utility in operations against guerrillas still seems open to question. To obtain meaningful results large areas have to be treated and in the tropics new growth appears distressingly quickly. Then too there are serious psychological and political drawbacks. The government's act of spraying poison from the air, no matter how carefully the flights are directed, is not likely to endear it to the population of the region concerned, and it gives the rebel propagandists a solid opportunity to play up the old themes of chemical and germ warfare. The insurgents are certain to blame all subsequent crop failures and epidemics on these tactics and a considerable number of people may believe them. This last is likely to be particularly true among the uneducated peoples of the backward areas where most guerrilla fighting takes place.

Even in more open and populated areas, a pilot's report that peasants are working in rice paddies is of little use to a headquarters which has no immediate way of telling whether or not the peasants are honest villagers or rebels. The same problems which complicate air observation are even more evident in using air power for attack against irregulars. In a form of warfare in which political considerations regularly outweigh the military, air attacks against "suspected enemy groups" are all too likely to be self-defeating. The loss of support brought on by each innocent man or woman killed is likely to far outweigh the possible gain of a hard-core rebel eliminated.

The speed of even the slowest fixed-wing aircraft is so great that the pilot has little chance of positively identifying an enemy who is not wearing a distinctive uniform, unless the latter obligingly waves a rifle or shoots at him. Even if he does this it is usually too late for the pilot to do more than turn for another pass, by which time the identified enemy, if he is prudent, will have disappeared.

The helicopter, which can maneuver easily or hover, gives the pilot a better chance to spot and attack a guerrilla on the ground, but here the problem of relative vulnerability becomes painfully acute.

Among the reasons why the Apache Indians under Geronimo were as formidable fighters as they were was that they realized, as the Plains Indians rarely did, that a man riding on a galloping horse and trying to shoot from the saddle at a dismounted and partly hidden enemy was fighting against very heavy odds. First, he had little chance of hitting his enemy. Second, a slight injury to himself or to his conspicuous mount could bring him down in a fall that would certainly take him out of the fight for a good while and might well be fatal. The Apaches fought dismounted and used their ponies for mobility.

The armed helicopter pilot is up against much the same problem. His target is not a well-defined trench line or convoy of trucks. He is after a scattered covey of individuals all seeking to make the most of the natural cover, and a good many of them firing back at him. There he sits, slow-moving and clearly outlined, like the tin duck in a shooting gallery, knowing that a hard hit on himself, the engine, the controls, or the rotors is likely to bring him down.

The helicopter is not really a direct attack vehicle. Its great value lies in its use as a small-unit transport, giving the soldiers it carries a mobility over any sort of terrain which the insurgents cannot hope to equal, and as a supply vehicle, carrying food and ammunition to troops in isolated areas and, when necessary, evacuating their wounded.

The development of modern weapons has changed many of the tactics of guerrilla warfare, but again their impact has been less here than on other forms of conflict. Nuclear weapons have no present application, and it seems unlikely that any foreseeable nuclear explosive device will have military advantages outweighing the immediate political damage of using it in an unconventional or guerrilla war. It may prove possible in the future to work out radioactive tracers to identify and tag individuals in contested areas or to lay down "hot" barriers against infiltration, but the public reaction to such gadgets may make them politically impractical even if they should prove to be technically feasible.

Most heavy weapons of war are equally inapplicable to guerrilla operations. Highly mobile groups of irregulars do not present much of a target for artillery fire, and guns, together with their ammunition, render the military forces more roadbound than ever. There may on occasion be use for light pack artillery or recoilless guns mounted on tracked vehicles or pack animals, but as a general rule the mules and the tractors can be put to better use carrying more prosaic cargoes such as men and food.

In the later stages of a guerrilla war, when the rebels have built up to the combat effectiveness of conventional troops, artillery may appear. The Greek Communists made some efforts to use heavy weapons, and even managed to shell Salonika for a period. Certainly a major factor in the fall of the French garrison in Dienbienphu near the end of the French campaign to hold what is now North Vietnam was the startlingly large concentration of field guns and antiaircraft which the Communists were able to throw into the fight. The French force was besieged in a position made up of a number of mutually supporting strong points which would have been more than adequate to hold off attacks by irregulars, and they held sufficient territory to permit easy support and resupply by airlift and parachute drop. But the training and supply of the Communist forces made them far more than guerrillas. Their guns, which had patently been brought south from China, were provided with a lavish amount of ammunition both to pound the ground positions and to render air operations in the area both difficult and expensive.

Over the years, the most important changes in the weaponry

of guerrilla war have stemmed from the progressive development
of modern small arms. Toward the end of the last century the
introduction of the magazine rifle and smokeless powder permitted men fighting from cover to deliver much increased fire
without immediately revealing their positions. This last was particularly important for the short, sharp exchanges in thick country which characterize much of guerrilla fighting. The Spanish
authorities became painfully aware of this during the Cuban
insurrection, and by the time of the Spanish-American War of
1898 the otherwise wretchedly equipped Spanish troops in Cuba
were largely armed with the modern Mauser rifle, while many
of the Americans opposing them still carried the old black-powder
Springfield.

Since then, the development and improvement of light machine guns, submachine guns, semiautomatic and automatic
rifles have continued to modify the tactics of guerrilla and counterguerrilla fighting, and as usual there have been gains and
losses for both sides.

Since automatic weapons so greatly increase the firepower of
any men using them, they have placed a new importance on
ambushes and surprise attack. Troops ambushed by even small
groups of guerrillas are likely to sustain heavy casualties before
they are able to return the fire. The saturating nature of automatic fire, particularly at close ranges, eases the requirement for
precision marksmanship in a surprise situation, and outside of
tribal areas in the Middle East marksmanship has rarely been a
guerrilla strong point.

All this helps the guerrilla, but there are some compensating
disadvantages. Ammunition consumption with automatic weapons is always high. With poorly trained men it is likely to be
astronomic. Guerrilla leaders are always concerned about ammunition shortages, and readers of Che Guevara's book will see that
for the Castro forces it was almost an obsession.

Fully automatic weapons, particularly submachine guns, are

extremely hard to control, and even if a half-trained man can be induced to fire short bursts instead of just blazing away, he is more than likely to throw most of his bullets far wide of the target. Forces which must capture most of their ammunition or have it infiltrated to them from the outside cannot afford this sort of profligacy very often.

After any fight, guerrillas make earnest efforts to recover all the empty brass cartridge cases they can find, for another disadvantage of automatic weapons is that their ammunition must be carefully and uniformly manufactured or the guns are likely to jam. Recapping and reloading ammunition is always a problem for irregulars in the field, but without the recovered cases, "do-it-yourself" ammunition production becomes just about impossible.

Then too, light machine guns and automatic rifles are in themselves fairly complex pieces of machinery, with close clearances in their moving parts. They must be well maintained, and for guerrillas, replacement of lost or broken parts for these guns often requires cannibalizing a badly needed weapon.

When rebels can count on extensive aid from the outside the problems of maintaining automatic weapons is greatly eased, but hardly ever completely solved. An exception appears to have been the Arab revolt, for T. E. Lawrence asserted that he had intentionally kept the Arab machine gunners ignorant of the inner workings of the weapons they served and instructed them to throw the guns away if they jammed, his theory being that the gunners could then continue in the attack using their rifles or sidearms, while they would be out of the fight completely if they stopped to strip and clear the gun.[1] If this practice was followed extensively, the British supply system must have been uniquely

[1] "Evolution of a Revolt," *The Army Quarterly*, No. 1, October 1920; reprinted in *Oriental Assembly* (edited by A. W. Lawrence) (London: Williams & Norgate, 1939), p. 126.

bounteous, and our own army has to take a back seat to the Arab irregulars when it comes to conspicuous military waste.

The military forces of the government have a far easier time maintaining and supplying their automatic weapons than do the guerrillas. Adequate ammunition is rarely a problem, and they have a far better opportunity to train their men in using and caring for their guns. Heavy machine guns, set up with cleared fields of fire, greatly strengthen the defenses of fixed points against guerrilla raids and permit relatively light garrisoning of defensive posts. Even in ambush situations where the guerrillas can make the best use of their automatic weapons, automatic fire from the survivors of the first attack may be sufficient to prevent the irregulars from closing in to seize supplies and weapons from the ambushed column. The soldier may not see his guerrilla enemy but, since ammunition conservation is not of primary importance to him, he can spray out fire to suppress the attack.

Indeed, the regular soldiers' ability to lay down suppressive fire at any threat of attack can have serious political consequences. Indiscriminate bursts of fire at indistinct and unidentified figures or at unusual sounds in the night can kill or wound enough innocent villagers and slaughter enough livestock to make the military cordially hated by the population.

One venerable weapon has been used in guerrilla operations for centuries and now appears to be as popular and effective as ever. This is the shotgun. Most irregular fighting in thick country takes place at short or point-blank ranges where the accuracy of a military rifle is wasted even in the hands of a well-trained man. Furthermore, much of the fighting takes place in the dark of night when accurate aiming is impossible. Under these circumstances a shotgun blast is likely to be pretty effective. The British issued large numbers of shotguns to the auxiliary forces they raised for village defense during the fighting in Malaya, and Castro's men used them extensively in the Cuban guerrilla operations.

Mortars have also proved useful in irregular operations. Troops have found them effective as antipersonnel weapons when guerrilla groups are located and pinned down, and rebels have used them to reduce defensive strong points without suffering prohibitive casualties. The Cubans devised a homemade mortar, consisting of a sawed-off shotgun with a bipod attached, which could hurl a Molotov cocktail, and equally impromptu high-trajectory weapons have been conjured up by other rebel movements.

Guerrillas have also found bazookas useful in ambushes, but these are rarely used, as in most cases they must be captured from the enemy troops. Regular soldiers have come to learn, moreover, that weapons such as bazookas and flame throwers are of relatively less use to them than they are to irregulars who may gain possession of them, so they are not often introduced into counterguerrilla operations.

In sum then, the introduction of modern infantry weapons into guerrilla war has made some changes in the tactics of both sides, but has not greatly altered the relative strengths of the regular and irregular opponents. The generally increased weight and rate of fire of new weapons certainly results in increased killing power, which at times is critically important, but it has a paradoxically weakening effect. Guerrillas, burdened with heavy items like mortar shells and increased quantities of required ammunition, tend to lose some of their precious mobility and freedom of movement. The government troops, carrying far larger loads of the same or heavier gear, tend to become even more roadbound than before. So the fight continues on much the same old terms.

VII

The Communist Approach to Unconventional War

We have already touched on many aspects of the Communist approach to unconventional warfare. However, it is important to see current and impending conflicts in terms of the over-all Communist philosophy of unconventional warfare and revolution. The actual course of events in any uprising is affected by many factors over which the rebels have little or no control, but the Communists do have very definite ideas on how they hope and intend a war of "liberation" to progress. Many Communist leaders have written on the subject, and certainly the most widely read and recognized of these authors is Mao Tse-tung, the now aging leader of the Chinese Communists. Mao's own accomplishments make him an unimpeachable authority, and his writings are studied exhaustively by most revolutionaries and would-be rebels. Today his works are receiving belated attention and careful examination in the military schools and staff colleges of the free world as well.

In essence, Mao envisages an insurgent war fought in three distinct and successive stages by three different categories of rebel forces. He predicates as the enemy a national government which is unpopular and increasingly bankrupt politically, although possessed of superior military strength, and he emphasizes repeatedly the cardinal importance of the rebels obtaining and holding the sympathy and support of the people as a whole.

Mao preaches that in the first stage of the revolt the outnumbered and militarily weak rebels refrain from open clashes with the stronger forces of the government and concentrate on planning and organizing the popular support that they will require as the movement matures. At this point, the rebellion is little more than a conspiracy. It may be built around a legal political party with nationally known figures at its head or it may be largely clandestine, but in either case, it does not at this stage constitute an immediate threat to the security of the government or the nation.

In Mao's second stage violence begins. Sabotage, assassinations of key government leaders at both national and local levels, and ambushes and raids on small military and police units become the order of the day. This is the stage of true guerrilla warfare. The insurgents still avoid open battle and try to limit the fighting to short, sharp attacks at times and places of their own choosing. They concentrate on building up their stocks of weapons, recruiting and at least partially training their new men, and they step up their efforts to convert, indoctrinate, and control the civil population. The necessary secure bases are established, either in remote areas or across some friendly border, and rebel authority is pushed outward to all parts of the country which the government forces are unable to occupy in strength. During this period the rebels will withdraw from any region where the government builds up its forces, returning when the troops are transferred elsewhere. This leads to the situation, seen in many unconventional campaigns, where much of the population finds itself under two alternating governments, paying taxes and providing supplies and recruits to whichever force controls their region at the moment.

Finally, if the government's strength is reduced by the strain of the guerrilla attacks and if the rebels are able to continue their political and military build-up, the insurrection moves into what Mao considers the third stage. Then the insurgent forces are sufficiently strong and well-trained to act as conventional troops, fighting the government's regular military forces on more or less even terms and holding territory by force of arms. The conflict then becomes a civil war in the classic sense, the guerrilla fighting is largely over, and the rebels have only to maintain the momentum of their growth to gain final and complete control of the country.

This, greatly abridged and simplified, is the Mao scenario for success in revolutions. The three categories of men that make up the revolutionary forces can also be described very briefly. First there is a hard core of the best trained, most experienced, and most dedicated men. From this group come the officers and political leaders of the movement. These men are full-time guerrillas. Through the early stages they are the organizers and teachers. They carry the brunt of the first violent operations, and those who survive the fighting are expected to be the leaders of the new government. As the insurrection progresses and the movement grows, some of these men will be drawn off for political and administrative duties and some will form the backbone for the military units the rebels will require as they move into stage three of the revolution.

The second category of men are the part-time guerrillas, who are initially recruited during stage one and serve in raid and ambush actions in their home districts during stage two. Far more numerous than the first category, these are not the elite of the revolution, and many of them will make up the rank and file of the military units formed during the last phase. The third category are hardly guerrillas and very far from being soldiers. Poorly trained militarily and poorly armed, they may be used for some combat operations in their immediate districts, but their main function is to provide support services for the fighting elements. These are the men who gather supplies, serve as couriers, collect intelligence, and aid in propaganda and indoctrination work. They are the immediate link between the active rebels and the people, and hence the political attitudes of the population are in large measure determined by the efficiency and effectiveness with which they do their work.

General Vo Nguyen Giap, the commander in chief of the North Vietnam Army, has also published his recipe for successful revolution,[1] and this closely parallels that of Mao. Giap also divides the campaign into three stages, but these are really further breakdowns of Mao's second and third stages, for Giap does not consider the preliminary period of planning, political organizing, and preparing for violent action a part of the battle itself. Like Mao, he places heavy and repeated emphasis on the rebels' need to gain full support of the people and to establish firm control over their activities.

He defines a stage of contention as the period of active guerrilla war, a stage of equilibrium as the period when the guerrillas are preparing to operate as conventional soldiers, and a stage of counteroffensive when the insurgents possess a true field army and are taking and holding territory. This is probably a sensible breakdown, as it highlights the transitional phase during which the insurgent movement is most vulnerable. This is when it finally attempts the transformation into a *de facto* government controlling a large, conquered area and conducting full-scale military operations.

As we have seen, much of the rebels' political strength and support stems directly from the peoples' belief that the rebellion represents the wave of the future. Once the revolutionary leaders present themselves as ready and able to protect their followers and their lands and to go after their enemy on even terms, they can reasonably expect a tremendous lift in their political prestige. At the same time they must face political and military tasks and

[1] *People's War, People's Army: The Viet Cong Insurrection Manual for Underdeveloped Countries.* Hanoi, North Vietnam: Foreign Languages Publishing House, 1961; New York: Frederick A. Praeger, 1962.

problems for which neither they nor their subordinates have had training or experience, the direction of a young nation engaged in open war. This is a great change from the shadow existence of the guerrilla period. New problems, new dangers, and new internal rivalries promptly become evident, and these produce strains unlike any the rebellion has encountered before.

But if the movement falters or suffers serious defeats or setbacks at this point it will lose its invaluable public image as the wave of the future. Minor, but evident military defeats will have incalculably damaging political effects. No insurrection can long stand still. If momentum is lost it must be quickly regained or a gradual decline is likely to begin, and this can hardly be arrested by anything short of a dramatic success.

Some rebellions have moved prematurely into Mao's third stage, have attempted fixed military action against government troops and, from the subsequent defeat, have drawn the _esprit_ and determination which led them to ultimate victory. An example of this, which I have already mentioned, occurred in 1916 when the Irish Republican Brotherhood seized and attempted to hold government buildings in the heart of Dublin. But it should be remembered that the Irish were fighting against a Western government already preoccupied with the problems of waging a worldwide war. When governments are not inhibited by any humane instincts, the fate of the Hungarian Freedom Fighters of 1956 is likely to be more typical.

Mao was fully aware of the difficulties of the transition from guerrilla to open warfare, but outside circumstances greatly eased the problem for the movement he led. Once the Chinese Communists completed their long march to the remote and vast areas of northwestern China, they enjoyed a freedom of maneuver and hence a security which few other regions could have given them. While he wrote often about the Japanese invader, and Chinese Communist forces did fight against the Japanese long and doggedly, the fact is that the Japanese were devoting most of their military energies to fighting the Nationalist Chinese and were regarded by the latter as their more immediate enemy. Thus Mao was able to expand his military efforts during the late thirties as the smaller participant in a large war, enjoying the reasonable certainty that neither of the other combatants could divert strong enough forces to destroy him. As the Second World War developed, the Chinese Communist received supplies and support as an element in the over-all Allied force, and by 1945 they were well into stage three of their revolutionary campaign; well equipped, well trained, battle hardened, and controlling a large area and population.

In Indochina, where the Vietminh rebellion against the French lasted from 1945 to 1954, Ho Chi Minh and his followers found the move from guerrilla war to what Giap called mobile war a far more difficult and taxing business. Through most of those years the French forces were strong enough to destroy any Vietminh units which accepted open battle. Hence Giap's natural emphasis on the stage of equilibrium, the transition between Mao's second and third stage. Only after the Communists gained complete control of the Chinese mainland in 1949 were the Vietminh rebels able to count on a sure refuge and source of supply to their north. From bases in southern China they were able to carry through the military build-up that finally enabled them to engage the French on equal terms and inflict the climactic defeat at Dienbienphu.

The parallels to the events of the American Revolution are far from exact and should not be stretched, but there are some interesting similarities. In the early years of the Revolution the Continental Army was far from strong. It achieved some successes, most notably Saratoga and the Trenton-Princeton campaign, but it had consistent difficulty in meeting the British regulars with the conventional military tactics of the day. The Americans held their own by fighting in their own way, and Sir John William Fortesque, in his *History of the British Army,* wrote of how the British troops "received the fire of the militia, who, safely posted behind trees, picked off officers, sergeants and corporals with unerring aim."[2] The great accomplishment of those years was keeping the rebellion alive and armed men in the field. The American revolutionists achieved a state of equilibrium some hundred and seventy years before General Giap coined the term. It was really not until France entered the war that the Continental Army received the supplies and foreign cooperation that permitted it to move into the stage of counteroffensive.

The Castro insurrection in Cuba was spared the third stage of that struggle by the convenient collapse of an already uncertain and unpopular regime. Guevara's book on that campaign is a fine study of many phases of guerrilla organization and tactics, but it leaves the reader with real doubts on how the Castro movement would have fared against a more imaginative and competent government. Guevara credits the Castro guerrillas with great courage and determination, and in this he is undoubtedly right, but he also makes it clear, perhaps unintentionally, that the Batista administration was a political and military patsy. It is not surprising that the collapse came as suddenly as it did.

Other guerrilla resistance movements have achieved their objectives without having to fight their way through Mao's third stage of open warfare. Two examples are the Irish Rebellion at the close of World War I and the Cyprus uprising of the early fifties. In these two cases the enemy was the British Government which, in this century at least, has been sensitive to world opinion and commendably reluctant to slaughter its subjects in large numbers. After determining that the rebel leaders possessed both the support of the population and the ability to set up a responsible administration, the British made the civilized decision to withdraw in good order. And the third stage of conflict was never reached.

[2] Vol. 3, p. 367 (London: Macmillan & Co., 1911).

The best illustration of a guerrilla resistance movement proceeding up to and through Mao's third stage to final success is probably that of Tito's success in Yugoslavia. Indeed, Tito's rise to power is almost a classic example of Mao's revolutionary progression. The first stage began long before the outbreak of World War II, and covered the organization of the Yugoslav Communist Party during the twenties and thirties. With the collapse of the Royal Yugoslav Government under the German attack of 1941, Tito was ready to move forward into the guerrilla fighting of stage two, and this he did after Germany attacked Russia in June of that year. Thereafter he was able gradually to expand the size and power of his partisan forces at the same time that he conducted operations both against the Germans and against the non-Communist Yugoslavs who might threaten his postwar position. While he received substantial aid from the Allies, Tito's consolidation of his political position and his build-up of military strength has to be recognized as a quite remarkable achievement.

Mao's arguments for three categories of revolutionaries in the insurgent movement are entirely logical, but here too, he is describing an arrangement which has worked well for revolutionaries through the years rather than presenting a new and original concept. In *The Seven Pillars of Wisdom*, T. E. Lawrence tells of the highly informal organization of the insurgent Arab force. There was a small elite group which served directly under the leaders of the revolt as bodyguards or personal troops. These units made up the permanent military hard core of the guerrilla force. They were supplemented by the warriors of the different Arab tribes involved in the rising. These came and went with a highly unmilitary freedom, and naturally were more in evidence when the fighting was in or near the regions that they knew best. Still, they were effective guerrillas and made up the bulk of the force. Finally, there were the villagers living on the fringes of the desert itself. These men fought when there was action in their immediate vicinity and demonstrated on several occasions that they could fight well, but their main function in the rising was to support the more active warriors and provide intelligence and occasional recruits. The military parallel to Mao's organizational structure is striking.

To return once more to the American Revolution, something of the same breakdown is found there. The hard core of the American force was the small but increasingly proficient Continental Army. Then there were militia regiments raised by the different states and serving relatively short enlistment periods. These appear to have been highly unpredictable outfits, sometimes fighting stubbornly and well as they did at Bennington during the Saratoga campaign, sometimes collapsing suddenly as did a number of units during the Battle of Camden in the south. As with all semitrained troops their performance depended directly on the quality of their leadership. Finally, there were the irregular and almost wholly informal local volunteers who provided most of their own weapons, made no pretense of military regularity and, with the startling exception of the fratricidal battle of King's Mountain, South Carolina, fought between units of this sort and American Tories in the British service, limited their activities to harassing, small-scale guerrilla operations. Thus, revolutionary wars have been fought for many years by rebel forces organized along the three levels of competence recommended by Mao.

It is certainly all to the good that the peoples of the free world are growing increasingly aware of the philosophy and doctrine on which the Communist leaders plan and conduct their unconventional campaigns. Still, there is danger that by relying too heavily on the Communist writers' helpful candor, we may attribute an undue rigidity to their methods. Although their long-term goal of achieving and consolidating Communist power remains constant, they have adopted some highly practical means of reaching that goal, and in the heat of their battles for power the Communists have been remarkably opportunistic.

Efforts to work out detailed theoretical blueprints of Communist aggression have proved of little value in forecasting their specific tactics in a particular situation. Remembering always that they have the double task of both gaining control of the country and of making it over in the Communist image, they are ready to exploit any weaknesses in the political, economic, or social fabric of the state. Since these weaknesses vary from country to country, it follows that the Communist appeals and attacks will vary as well. Here again we see the tremendous advantage they gain from controlling a well-organized, disciplined, and politically perceptive Communist Party within the target country. An insurgent movement which initiates guerrilla operations against an unpopular government can, in its early stages, gain much of its needed popular support by identifying with elements in the population already restive, and by espousing genuine grievances. Virtually all intelligent rebel leaders have acted on this sound and obvious principle.

The Communists envisage that the same heavily indoctrinated and disciplined group which leads the rebellion through the guerrilla stage will form the backbone of the governmental bureaucracy once the battles are won and a Communist regime takes over. From these men will be chosen the Party leaders, the provincial administrators, and the security police officers who will reshape the society and economy of the country in the Communist image. This succession of duties fits well with the Communist concept that the masses should be controlled and guided by a small elite. In differing circumstances and at different stages of the revolution the same trained and tested Communist Party member may play the roles of conspirator, military hero, civil administrator, and ruthless enforcer.

The double role of saviour and captor, the combined use of the carrot and the stick, presents the Communist leaders with some very delicate political decisions. Since each situation must be met as it arises, and the Communist line is greatly influenced by the position taken by the authorities, it becomes all the harder to foretell the exact course of any rebellion.

There is, however, one trend which seems to be a constant for all Communist insurrections. As the guerrilla fighting proceeds and the rebel movement matures, there is increasing emphasis on terror and coercion as the primary means of guiding and controlling the population. If the revolutionary movement is successful, as in Yugoslavia, Cuba, and French Indochina, the weakening authorities have less and less chance of swinging meaningful popular support to their side. Few if any of the people wish to identify themselves closely with the losing side. At the same time the insurgents' position becomes progressively more secure, and they no longer have to concern themselves so urgently with winning and holding the wholehearted support of all the people. Therefore they are able to get on with the other half of their over-all objective—that of changing the face and nature of the national society. On the other hand, in cases where the insurrection is obviously losing headway and faces ultimate defeat, the rebels have progressively less chance of securing voluntary support and assistance from the people. By mid-1949, for example, the Greek Communist guerrillas found themselves in this position. Hence, during the waning months of a rebellion its leaders have no alternative but to seize what support and supplies they can, and they come to depend increasingly on terror and coercion.

This violent last act of the drama does not appear in the Communist writings, for they cannot allow of the possibility of failure. Nevertheless, it is a very real factor in fighting unconventional campaigns and must be foreseen and prepared for by the authorities.

VIII

The Government under Unconventional Attack

Governments, like individuals, react to stress and danger in widely different ways, and the reactions are frequently unpredictable. A teacher giving a final examination or a junior officer, taking his unit into action for the first time, may feel he knows his men well, but he invariably has a few surprises when some perform notably well and others show unexpected weaknesses. So it is with armies and nations as a whole. The swift collapse of France under the German attack of 1940 contrasted sharply with the brilliant performance of the Greeks when the Italian forces tried to gobble them up later in the same year.

The difference between a nation's success or its ignominious failure often depends on the clarity and urgency with which its people see their danger. While much of this understanding depends on what the leaders say and do, the most clear-cut threat will evoke the strongest and most unified response. The starkly obvious nature of the peril facing Britain during that same year of 1940 helped her to concentrate the energy she needed to win through. Each Briton could see that his nation had to hold off a strong and hitherto victorious enemy or go down, and for the time being nothing else mattered.

When the threats, external or internal, confronting a country are not so evidently dangerous nor so easily identified, it is infinitely more difficult for the leaders to call forth the same dedication and unity of effort. Lesser difficulties create pressures and strains that tend to exacerbate the class, religious, or racial tensions which would be muted by a more overwhelming threat. The rivalries and disputes of normal political and commercial life are, if anything, accentuated, and under these circumstances it is well-nigh impossible to bring the full strength of a democratically governed state to bear on its problems. We saw something of this in the United States during the Korean War which, while a demanding and important conflict, did not immediately threaten our national survival. Coming just five years after our smashing victories over Japan and Germany, the frustrations of struggling in that distant and barren land produced a national neurosis which will puzzle historians for years to come. The leaders who made the tough but inescapable decision to fight open Communist aggression were at the same time denounced for involving us in war and accused of being soft on Communism. We fought the Korean War with a sense of bewilderment and uncertainty as to our objectives that was wholly new to us, and the rights and wrongs of the negotiated settlement were long and actively debated.

In much the same fashion, an economic depression has an essentially divisive impact on a nation. A general agreement that things are not as they should be is combined with bitter disagreement on what should be done to remedy matters, and again it takes a high quality of leadership to call forth anything like unified national action.

Unconventional aggression presents a painfully complex combination of challenges to the government under attack for, as we have seen, it strikes at the social, economic, and military foundations of the state. Furthermore, during the early stages of the assault none of the problems created, taken singly, seem to warrant extensive and burdensome countermeasures.

The authorities, confronted by a gradually rising tide of subversive propaganda and public disorder along with occasional political assassinations, are likely to feel that precipitate countermeasures will be interpreted as signs of insecurity and panic, lending the incipient rebellion a dignity and importance that it should not possess. The temptation is, therefore, to meet each incident as a separate problem, playing down the significance of the general unrest. If this policy is followed in the face of a well-organized rebellious movement, the authorities inevitably find themselves running out of thumbs to stop holes in the dike, and the whole structure begins to weaken.

If the government, and the nation, is fortunate it will have competent leaders to meet the worsening situation, but as we have seen, Communist unconventional offensives are usually directed against those states where the leadership is most inexperienced, inadequate, or insecure. The government's reaction to the attack is all too likely to be either inadequate or inappropriate, and the opportunity to arrest the insurrection quickly and relatively painlessly may be missed.

Even when a rebellion has moved well into Mao's second stage, and the country is racked with full-scale guerrilla war, the government is often reluctant to take the full measures necessary to put a stop to its troubles. This reluctance may stem from an obtuse, but honest, failure to appreciate how serious matters have become, but in many instances, adequate measures are not taken even when the emergency is recognized for what it is. There may be many reasons for this, but three are most commonly encountered.

First, counterguerrilla operations are both expensive and highly inconvenient. The army must leave the relative comfort and tranquillity of barracks life for the toughest and most demanding form of campaigning. Many of the army leaders cling to the traditional concept that their task is to protect the nation from military invasion, and there is a strong temptation to leave bandit hunting to the police.

Then too the political and economic aspects of counterguerrilla campaigns may be hard for a weak government to face up to. Popular reforms, particularly land reforms, involve taking privilege or property or both from those previously holding them. In traditional societies the privileged and propertied usually possess the power to promote or temporarily to prevent change, and so their carrying through such reforms stems either from enlightened self-interest or desperation. In the early stages of an unconventional aggression the national leaders are not likely to be desperate, and in too few cases are they farsighted enough to see the great advantage of broadening their base of political support. Thus half measures are adopted, and the unrest which supports the rebellion continues unabated.

Second, in a revolutionary situation the rebel leaders have usually worked hard and long to identify themselves with popular grievances, and the authorities are often reluctant to make the reforms needed to meet these grievances for fear that they will appear to be making concessions to the rebels out of weakness. In these cases the government's official policy line is usually that reforms will be considered and granted only after the insurgents have been defeated and peace restored. The authorities then concentrate on the police and military operations which they hope will smother the disaffection and try to postpone political action until later.

It has been demonstrated again and again in unconventional wars that this government policy is the highroad to disaster. The government locks itself into the stand-pat position of fighting to defend all the inequities which gave the rebellion its original impetus. No matter how sincere and well intentioned the leaders may be in their statements on future improvements, they are inevitably judged by their actions, and so long as the fighting continues they are cast as the forces of reaction. This was the position in which Chiang and the other leaders of Nationalist China were placed in the years after World War II—a period when they were far better situated than the Chinese Communists to build up the strength and well-being of the Chinese people.

This sort of government policy greatly simplifies the propaganda task of the insurgents. They are able to offer all varieties of pie in the sky for the days after they come to power, because the government gives them no sort of realistic competition. Of course the Communist propagandists will make any and all assurances of a future heaven on earth which they feel will be credible, but these appeals will be considerably blunted if the people can see for themselves that the government is really improving their lot in the here and now.

As a guerrilla insurrection continues, and the people see that the government is not taking positive steps to retain their loyalty and support, they become increasingly willing to stand the deprivations and misery of a war situation, for they begin to believe the rebel propagandists' assertions that only through painful struggle will they be able to meet their needs and aspirations. Then too, the longer a government defers reforms or concessions, the more will be demanded in the end. For example, if a British government had been able to work out a system for home rule in Ireland before the beginning of the war in 1914, the history of the Irish Rebellion would have been far different. By 1918 no such arrangement was possible. The struggle was then too bitter, the breach too wide. Probably the same is true of our own Revolution. If George III and Lord North had better gauged the temper of the American Colonies and changed their policies, the Declaration of Independence might never have been written. Of course, these analogies are not arguments for concessions and compromise with Communist expansion. The point is that any government not based entirely on police power must justify its own worth and value to the people it governs.

There is a third reason why the leaders of weak and underdeveloped states are often slow to respond effectively to unconventional aggressions. This is that they are often reluctant to

seek help from stronger allies and friends in meeting this form
of attack. When a nation is openly invaded by a hostile alien
army it is entirely natural and honorable for the government to
call on friendly powers for aid in fighting off the attack. Indeed,
this is what alliances are for. On the other hand, if a government
is buffeted by uprisings of its own subjects it is much more of a
family affair, and a cry for outside help is tantamount to an admission of impotence. Even if the revolt is put down with the
aid of foreign soldiers, the future position of the government is
seriously compromised for its main mandate to rule is the power
of another government's bayonets. Therefore, while the threatened leaders will almost certainly welcome material aid and
diplomatic backing, they have to be in desperate straits before
they welcome the appearance of foreign troops.

This is why it has proved so critically important to demonstrate beyond a shadow of doubt that the Communist-inspired
guerrilla risings threatening the weaker nations of the free world
are in fact inspired, supported, and guided from the Communist
powers. Once it is demonstrated and generally accepted that a
nation is under unconventional assault from beyond its own
borders, much of the stigma of accepting friendly intervention
and assistance is removed.

Even under these circumstances it is difficult for the leaders
of newly independent countries to lean too heavily on Western
powers for guidance and support in meeting unconventional
aggression. There is still more vitality in the political issue of
colonialism than most Westerners, particularly Americans, are
likely to realize. Where the guerrilla rebels are largely indigenous, and a good number of them are fighting within a few miles
of the villages where they were born, even the most law-abiding
citizens recognize a continuing bond with them. The appearance
of government troops guided, advised, and supported by Cau-
casians who speak strange tongues and eat strange rations is
likely to wake old and unpleasant memories.

Fear of these reactions, together with a natural and commendable desire to demonstrate their ability to solve their own problems without conspicuous participation by outsiders, leads many leaders to belittle the threat to their country or to delay accepting direct support from a Western power, even when they fully realize that the assault against them is directed and sustained by an outside enemy.

These are the difficulties which inhibit prompt and effective government action. They must be borne in mind while we consider the tasks which the authorities must face and accomplish if they are to defeat the attack being made on their country. The urgent need is to identify the government firmly with the needs and the aspirations of the people, for this is the only way to build a solid base of voluntary and wholehearted support.

It is, of course, far easier for the national leaders to pay lip service to this concept than to put it into real effect. If they are to be successful they must carry through at much the same time four distinct and far-reaching programs.

First there is the matter of redress of grievances, which has already been mentioned above. Obviously no nation, particularly one which is underdeveloped and subjected to serious strains, can transform itself into a prosperous garden spot overnight, but positive and well-publicized steps have to be taken to improve existing conditions. To people whose whole experience is centered in the fields around a country village or in the factories and slums of a few blocks of a great city, small changes for the better can be vastly significant—far more compelling than airy promises of vast changes which reach beyond the limits of their comprehension. Removal, or even amelioration of official corruption at local levels is perhaps as important as anything. Mao, Giap, and Guevara all emphasize the critical importance of the guerrilla paying for all that he takes from the citizenry during the early stages of a revolt. The civil or military official who is any less scrupulous merely aids the cause of the rebels. Magsaysay drove this point home to the Philippine Army when he first became Secretary of Defense in that country, and the cause of the Huk insurgents began to decline from the day when the Philippine citizen came to realize that the appearance of government troops did not threaten his crops, his livestock, and his poultry. The honest collection of taxes is a major step in correcting and improving the image of the government in the eyes of the people. Even more important is the matter of land reform in areas where this is a major grievance. As we have seen, this is a slow and difficult program to put into full operation, but a few concrete steps which lend credence to the government's assertions of good intent will work wonders.

Improved public health provisions, improved schools, better roads and communications are all part of the same program, and each move will help both in actually improving the standard of living and productivity of the people and in convincing them of the government's genuine concern and interest in their welfare.

At the same time the military aspects of the problem must be vigorously met, or the political effort will have little meaning or effect. Here there are three related but distinct jobs to be done. The first is the active pursuit and destruction of the guerrilla units in the field. We have already examined some of the requirements and problems of these operations, and it is enough here to re-emphasize that the primary objective is not to destroy the guerrillas by inflicting casualties, it is rather to make further armed rebellion unprofitable and hopeless and thus pave the way for the rebels' gradual return into the normal society of the country.

A second aspect of the military problem is the far more complex and politically loaded task of denying the guerrilla forces access to the population. Only when the two are effectively isolated from each other can the rebel be cut off from the supplies, recruits, and intelligence which we have seen he requires, or can the potentially loyal elements of the population be protected from depredation and coercion. Some of the difficulties here are unchanging and appear in revolution after revolution. How can the static defense of important fixed points be assured without hopelessly tying down the greater part of the military force? This puzzled Napoleon's armies in their struggle with the guerrillas of Spain, and it was still troubling the French Army when the Algerian struggle drew to a close. Related to this is the question of whether it is safe to organize and arm local units in the hope that they can take over some of the onerous fixed-point defense work. The French armed a number of Vietnamese units only to have the men desert, with their weapons, to the Viet minh. During the American Revolution Cornwallis provided equipment to Tory militia and later saw some of this gear used against him. Nevertheless, unless the people can defend themselves or be protected, they cannot be expected to cooperate with the authorities. This is the rationale behind the strenuous efforts being made today in South Vietnam to set up workable systems of village defense.

There is obviously no pat answer to these problems. If the military were adequately strong and the populace adequately loyal to perform both functions, the guerrilla insurrection would not be a threat and all would soon be well. Furthermore, there is no sure formula to determine the best approach for the authorities to take. The factors of relative material and moral strength vary from country to country and shift during each state of a rebellion. The only solid and unchanging fact is that a guerrilla force pushed onto the defensive is in deep trouble if it cannot promptly regain the initiative. No government ever defeated a rebellion by purely defensive tactics.

The third military job is to cut off the rebels from sources of supply outside the country. This is frequently the most difficult task of all. Where a border runs through jungle or mountainous country, it is virtually impossible to block all trails and byways. This has been the situation in Laos and South Vietnam, and the borders of many of the states of both Latin America and central Africa are equally porous. Even where a national frontier runs through relatively open country, the very length of the border may make it impossible for the government forces to patrol it effectively, particularly when those forces are already under heavy pressure elsewhere. A long coastline presents many of the same difficulties. The recent nationalist Algerian insurrection presents a case in point here, for the French forces were never able to prevent extensive infiltration, either across the Mediterranean shoreline or over the long borders with Tunisia and Morocco.

Failure to interdict traffic of this sort is not necessarily a reflection on the quality or determination of the government forces. Eastern Europeans continue to work their way through the Iron Curtain, and during Prohibition we were conspicuously incapable of stopping rumrunning on a large scale. When such activities have the backing and support of a powerful government, they are all the harder to prevent.

Simultaneously with its civil reforms and military operations the government must also mount an extensive information campaign of propaganda and education. Too often this program is viewed as merely an effort to counter the propaganda put out by the rebels and by radio stations in neighboring countries which are supporting their cause. To be fully effective such a program has to do a great deal more than that.

As we have seen, the government of an underdeveloped nation being subjected to unconventional attack is actually fighting two wars. One is to defeat the immediate threat posed by the guerrillas. The other is to carry the country through the turmoil and frustrations of modernization and early industrialization. This second struggle would take place whether the guerrillas existed or not, and is merely complicated by their presence. Still, unless the people can be convinced of both the feasibility and the advantages of winning the long-run fight to develop the nation and improve their own welfare, they will not have the motivation and the determination to beat off the revolutionary aggression. In short, the advantages of potential long-term gain must be held out as the reason and the reward for defeating the short-term threat.

To this end the government has to explain its programs in ways which are both understandable and credible to the mass of the population. These programs and their results must appear sufficiently attractive and attainable to make the people identify their own hopes for the future with the survival of the government rather than with its overthrow and removal. It takes a high order of salesmanship to get this message across to an apathetic and largely uneducated population whose previous contacts with a distant central government may well have been limited to corrupt tax collectors and rapacious soldiery. However, if the authorities cannot make their position clear and compelling, they cannot hope to call forth the willingness to fight and to sacrifice without which no war can be won. Their only hope then is that the rebels will so mismanage their campaign and so alienate the people that the old regime will be protected as the lesser of two evils. This is hardly a promising prospect.

If the government leaders are able to evoke the positive loyalty and support of the majority their position is greatly strengthened, but achieving this is only a part of what the propaganda and educational campaign must do. As was pointed out earlier, the granting of any privilege involves its withdrawal from someone else, and in lands where privilege and wealth are highly concentrated, this means that the immediate and apparent losers in a period of reform are either part of or close to the leadership group itself. They usually include the large landholders, a good part of the military officer corps, and the upper bureaucracy and most of whatever commercial class exists. Therefore the government is pushed into some fine political tightrope-walking. If the form and progress of the reforms are not adequate the mass of the people may shift toward supporting the rebels. On the other hand, if the need for the reforms is not understood by the propertied classes or if the changes seem excessive to them, there are likely to be splits within the leadership group, with accompanying dangers of *coups d'état* and palace revolutions.

This appears to be the situation in a number of nations today. Iran is perhaps a good example. The top leadership is pushing development plans and programs in the face of considerable internal opposition but is being pressed by events and by popular feeling to move ahead still faster. In these circumstances the government's propaganda and educational campaign has to include convincing explanations to its own elite of the need for measures which the conservatives may feel smack of the very socialist programs that the rebels are advocating.

Here again is the difficulty of bringing a unified national effort to bear on the country's troubles, which many of the people at all levels in the society do not as yet take seriously. The educational program must be multibarreled, for each economic and social stratum must be led to see the advantages of positive loyalty.

And so the propagandist's life is not a happy one. In addition to meeting and solving the above difficulties, he must walk two other difficult figurative tightropes.

One is how best to handle the vexing problems of rising popular expectations for the future. While the government spokesman must compete in reasonable measure with the rebel propagandist who is promising the moon to all who will support the insurrection, he is painfully hampered by having to stick to the facts or something very like them. The people know that the government has the authority, and they assume that it has the power to make good on its promises of better administration and better times for all, but they appreciate that guerrilla prophecies of a golden age can only be put to the test if and when the guerrillas become the government. If the authorities arouse hopes they must make good on them in a reasonable time or face disastrous popular disillusionment.

Then another neat problem is posed by the need to impress the people with the real danger to the nation without inducing panic or despair. We have seen that much of the momentum of a Communist insurrection stems from the Communists' constantly repeated assertion that they represent the political wave of the future. If the authorities say anything which may alarm the people in this regard, they are only fighting themselves. The government spokesman is in the position of a doctor who must persuade a nervous and seriously ill patient to stay in bed and take his medicine without at the same time putting him in fear of his life.

In the last analysis, the government's information and indoctrination program has to be built on simple and direct themes. It can explain the government's long-term plans and intentions for the development of the country and the benefit of the people. It can demonstrate what is being done to further these plans. It can call for cooperation and support in preventing the rebels from impeding and wrecking these plans. If the government does indeed have a feasible and attractive program and is clearly working hard to put it into effect, these appeals can have great impact.

Fourthly and finally, the government must concentrate on protecting and developing the nation's economy. This is often the most difficult aspect of countering an unconventional attack, for not only are political and military countermeasures woefully expensive but, as we have seen, the rebels make every effort to disrupt the country's economic life. It is in this field that small and already weakened nations most urgently need help from stronger and more affluent friends. But simply securing adequate funds is far from enough. Again thoughtful planning and strong leadership are required. The stresses of unconventional war are felt by every individual at every level in the economy, and financial injections to the body politic have to be distributed to ease the pain throughout. The balance must be made between stepping up progress on long-term operations and meeting immediate needs. Allocating and spending large sums of money during a crisis period, when accountings and reviews are likely to be sketchy at best, increases the temptations toward corruption and mismanagement at just the time and in just the places where the authorities must prove their integrity and patriotism.

In sum, the government must find the resources, human and material, simultaneously to conduct a hard war and to carry through far-reaching changes in the social and economic life of the nation. In today's rapidly changing world few of the underdeveloped states can do this alone and unaided. Making the most effective use of any aid provided inevitably calls for foresight, care, and, occasionally, discretion, but the sooner the authorities recognize and acknowledge that appropriate help is needed, the better is their chance of winning through and retaining their independence.

IX

The Government under Unconventional Attack: Some Political Problems

Like a patient whose resistance has been worn down by long illness, a government fighting off an unconventional aggression is peculiarly susceptible to secondary infections which threaten it still further. Two of these threats are particularly important.

One is the danger of a breakdown in the working relationships between the civil and military leaders of the nation. We in this country tend to forget how remarkably unstable this relationship is in most of the underdeveloped countries of the world. The firm principle of civilian control over the military was incorporated in the United States Constitution, and we have operated on this basis throughout our national history. There have been occasional clashes such as the one that led to the recall of General MacArthur from Korea, but the principle of civilian direction has always been reaffirmed. Few if any of the nations now threatened by unconventional aggression have such a binding tradition, and the unstable civil-military relationship becomes particularly precarious when a government must use military force to battle insurgents within the nation's population.

As we have seen the political and military aspects of such a battle become inextricably intertwined. Whether or not he wishes it, the military leader finds himself deep in politics, and the civil leader must incorporate urgent military considerations in all his plans and programs. Each group is thus forced to work in the other's field in a way which could hardly occur while fighting a conventional war against a foreign enemy. In these circumstances, many military men have been bitterly disillusioned by the inadequacies of their civilian colleagues, and groups of officers have seized control in a number of countries. For Americans, the military take-over of the South Korean Government is probably the most familiar example of such a move.

In many cases these officers can make a good case that they are well qualified to manage national affairs, for they are frequently among the best-educated and most sophisticated men in the country. Many, particularly from former colonial areas, have attended war colleges and staff schools in the United States or in Europe. As a result they are well-traveled, experienced at working with foreigners, and able to view the problems of their nation with an objectivity and perspective which few of their civilian counterparts can match.

In most instances the officer corps is recruited almost entirely from the social and economic elite of the country and has always felt itself a part of the governing class. These soldiers' attitude toward their participation in the daily political life of their countries reflects something of the approach of the earlier colonial regimes before the regions became independent. In their colonies, Britain, France, and, to a somewhat lesser extent, America blended the civil and military aspects of administration, and in many posts civilians and soldiers were virtually interchangeable. In the Spanish colonies the distinction was hardly made at all. Not unnaturally something of this attitude rubbed off on the former colonials and influences their thinking today.

There is no question that in many instances the soldiers have sharply improved the administration of affairs. Their training and experience have enabled these leaders to mobilize the national effort to meet internal crises or unconventional aggression, and for the short run the governments may be much strengthened, as appears to have been the case in South Korea. For the long run, however, a system that makes the trains run on time and rules through various forms of martial law is far from satisfactory. The rigidity and arbitrary quality of virtually all military administrations tend to inhibit the ferment of ideas and new concepts which are at the core of all modernization.

It is true that in periods of crisis and danger when unity of action is essential, some special restraints may have to be placed on political opposition. At the peak of the American Civil War Lincoln found it advisable temporarily to suspend habeas corpus, but the national elections of 1864 were held on schedule. However, in states where the philosophy and processes of democratic government are new and are often imperfectly understood, leaders in difficult times are easily tempted to consider all opposition to their policies as dangerous and subversive. Unhappily, there appear to be marked signs of this sort of thinking in the government of South Vietnam today. When this happens the administration's ability to work with and to accept suggestions from outside its own ranks decreases, and the government tends to slide closer and closer to the dictatorial pattern. To the extent that power corrupts the leaders, their eagerness to put an end to the disturbances that brought them to power tends to diminish, and they seek ways to perpetuate their authority.

There have been some honest and commendable efforts by military leaders to take power only long enough to set the nation on what they believe to be the right track and then to withdraw in favor of civil leadership. Burma, Turkey, and Argentina are all examples. But in each case the army seems to have found the civilian authorities unequal to what it considers to be the task and is drawn back recurrently into political affairs. The military officers who seized control of the South Korean Government in the *coup d'état* of May 1961 also professed the intention to return the country to civil control as soon as possible. In the first communiqué issued by the Military Committee after the revolution the members stated that they would "transfer power to new and conscientious politicians as soon as our mission has been completed, and return to our original duties." As of this writing, the makeup of the committee has changed, but the country is still under firm military rule. We now see military governments in many states of the Middle East and Latin America. Furthermore, there is the strong likelihood that others will appear in the new states of Africa.

In each of these cases of military rule it is easy to point out the inadequacies of the earlier civil regimes which led the soldiers to displace them, but it is not so easy to see how future civilian leadership will be nurtured under the existing system. Gradual transformations may take place but, in the meanwhile, the political maturing of the countries concerned toward truly stable systems of government is definitely impeded and delayed.

Throughout the centuries military governments have appeared in many states not subject to unconventional aggression from beyond their borders, but the breakdown of working relationships between military and civil authorities which paves the way for military take-over is particularly likely to occur when governments are under this form of attack. It can only be prevented if both groups of leaders share a mutual respect and a common objective. It is a primary task of top government leadership to assure that this community of interest and purpose is created and maintained. Direct military participation in the government of the threatened nations is likely to be far broader than we would consider suitable or acceptable in a long-established Western democracy, but where talent and experience are both desperately needed and in short supply, good men must be used wherever they can be most useful.

Another secondary infection which threatens a government in the grip of an unconventional attack becomes particularly serious during the period of convalescence. This is the problem of rehabilitating the former guerrillas and their more ardent supporters as law-abiding members of a peaceful community. By their very nature guerrilla wars cannot be brought to a tidy solution with a dramatic signing of documents on the deck of a battleship. Authorities who are getting the best of a rebellion of this sort can only measure their progress toward victory in fragmentary statistics and a gradually changing atmosphere in the country as a whole. The number of ambushes, raids, and assassinations tapers off. The people begin to give information against the guerrillas more freely and more openly. Guerrilla losses in both men and material mount, and an increasing number of rebels turn themselves in and surrender. No guerrilla movement with a high desertion rate can hope either to operate effectively or to long survive. For practical purposes, its back is broken.

But paradoxically the question of how to handle a waning guerrilla insurrection is a difficult one for the government, both from the political and military points of view. Militarily, the law of diminishing returns begins to operate against the authorities, for the last hard-core guerrillas are always the most difficult to kill or capture. The number of troops required and the number of casualties likely to be suffered in the process seem out of all proportion to the gains of rounding up relatively small numbers of men who are reduced to little more than armed and desperate fugitives. If a weary nation, already relieved of its worst pressures, sees a continuing and costly operation with little visible return, it may well begin to have new doubts about the wisdom and efficiency of its government.

On the other hand, the surrendered guerrilla is a tricky problem in himself. In arousing the people to fight off the rebellious attack, the government has repeatedly emphasized that the guerrillas are evil and dangerous criminals working in a treasonous cause. After months and years of following this line, it is awkward to shift and try to reintroduce the individual member of the criminal movement into law-abiding society without punishing him for his deeds.

Governments confronted with this problem have followed different courses and the results are worth considering. During the

Korean War the government of South Korea usually treated each former member of the Communist-led guerrilla bands as a criminal by the very fact of his membership, and it appears that offers of amnesty were not always scrupulously honored. The most obvious result of this policy was an extremely low surrender rate. Some of the guerrillas fighting in the hills of South Korea at the end of formal hostilities were dedicated, hard-core Communists who were well-nigh immune to any inducements, but at least an equal number of men had come into the guerrilla forces opportunistically, in error or under duress. They would have been happy to stop fighting, but could see no way of returning to their old life. Understandably, these men preferred to continue their precarious life as bandits to turning themselves in to face a firing squad or a labor camp.

In the Philippines and in Federation of Malaya the authorities followed the opposite course and, as we have seen, the results fully justified their decision. The official statements of these governments and all the propaganda directed either to the population as a whole or to the guerrillas themselves drove home the point that there could be no compromise or agreement with the rebellious movement itself. It was intolerable, and the government was determined to crush it. At the same time a very different approach was made to the individual members of the guerrilla movement. Everything was done to convince them that there really was a golden bridge over which they could return to peaceful life. They would, of course, have to face trial for crimes which they had personally committed, just as they would in ordinary civil life, but the simple fact that they had joined the guerrilla movement and had fought against the government did not automatically make them permanent outlaws. Total absolution for individual sins would have been a little too much for the peaceful and long-suffering citizenry to have stomached, but the realization that men could come back from the jungle to start a new life and that a number were doing just that gave the public a different concept of the Communist guerrilla force. They no longer appeared as a dedicated army. Rather, they became a group of ragged rowdies who were giving up their original high-flown ideas and were throwing themselves on the mercy of a beneficent government.

The authorities still have to take into consideration two potential dangers in granting amnesties and, especially, rewards to surrendering guerrillas. The first is that loyal citizens who supported the government through the worst of the uprising and may have suffered severely in consequence may hotly resent too tolerant treatment of former rebels. This danger is likely to be more apparent than real and, in the Philippines at least, there was less resentment than the government had at first anticipated. Then too, if the decline in the rebellion brings with it a steady improvement in conditions, the country is likely to be in a generally forgiving mood.

The second consideration in the granting of amnesties and rewards is one of timing and scale. Massive efforts to buy off the guerrillas while the rebellion is in full swing are likely to be unsuccessful and, worse still, may smack of the ancient British custom of paying the Danegeld, the tribute which the Saxon kings of England periodically paid to buy off the Danish raiders who threated to ravage the eastern coasts of Britain. This danger can be averted by emphasizing the distinction between the guerrilla movement and the individual member, and by moving the program into high gear only when it has become evident that the insurgent attack has been effectively slowed down.

In sum, it is certainly safe to say that considered efforts to encourage guerrilla surrenders with genuine and generous offers of rehabilitation and new opportunities in peaceful life have paid off wherever they have been tried.

X

Foreign Support of Insurrection: In Free Countries

Aggressive nations have always furthered their foreign policies by careful efforts to determine and exploit their neighbors' weaknesses. These weaknesses can often be compounded by diplomatic or economic pressures and by saber rattling. When feasible, a third nation or group has sometimes been exploited to exert the pressure or to carry the brunt of the fighting if actual war breaks out. France made excellent use of this technique in using the North American Indian tribes to harass British colonial frontiersmen during the Seven Years' War. Not surprisingly, that part of the war is generally referred to in America as the French and Indian War.

Obviously, the leaders of an aggressive nation find it even more convenient and economical if they can persuade citizens of the state they wish to attack to espouse their cause and to fight the matter out with their own countrymen. The foreign aggressor can then provide limited amounts of aid to the faction it favors and thereby has a good chance of gaining control over the situation at little or no cost to itself. As we have seen, the Communist states have frequently tried to use the national Communist parties of the free world in just this way.

It is important to remember, however, that the motives and objectives of the indigenous leaders of a rebellion may differ drastically from those of the foreign government aiding them in their fight. The indigenous insurgent leaders have but one primary objective. This is to win their war and seize control. Their strategy and tactics are shaped to gain this end, and they view any happening elsewhere in terms of its effect on the immediate fortunes of their campaign. Readers of Mao Tse-tung's writings appreciate that he was fully abreast of world events during his struggle for power, but it is clear that he considered the Sino-Japanese fighting in the nineteen thirties and even World War II as secondary events taking place off stage, important only as they furthered or thwarted his efforts. In the same sense, many of the Greek rebels of the late forties were dedicated believers in the concept of communism. They were doubtless concerned at the damage to Communist world unity when Tito defected from Moscow in 1948, but they were certainly more acutely dismayed at the blow to their own future prospects.

The Soviet leaders and now to a lesser extent the Chinese, must view events from the far broader perspective forced on them by their own success as revolutionaries. They are responsible for the whole destiny of powerful nations, and the progress of one unconventional campaign against a country of the free world has to be balanced in with multitudinous other national interests and ambitions. Therefore, the direction and support given to the hard-pressed leaders of a national insurrection may be ill suited to these leaders' personal hopes and urgent needs.

The relationships between the sponsor nation and the supported guerrilla is almost inevitably a difficult one. Fully effective cooperation between the two calls for a high order of dedication and discipline on the part of the rebel, who carries the full strain of the fighting and whose life is at stake, as well as a real appreciation of his difficulties by those who are supporting him. Usually the insurgent in the field comes to suspect that he is being exploited and starved of needed support, while the sponsor begins to feel that the fighting man harbors suspiciously independent and ungrateful tendencies. While each has some measure of control over the other, the position of the outside supporting state is far the stronger of the two. The guerrilla can rarely hope to survive if support is withdrawn from him.

Yet the outside sponsor may well find his other interests lead him to cut off the resistance he has encouraged. If the sponsor does abandon a rebellion which he has incited and supported from the outside, he inevitably strikes a cruel blow to the fortune and future of the rebels involved, and this calls for a form of amoral ruthlessness which sits far more easily on the Communist than on the Western conscience. Still, Western states have done this under the strain of war. Mikhailovitch received the support of the Allied powers during the earlier days of World War II, but this support was withdrawn when it became apparent that a choice would have to be made between him and Tito, and the choice was made on the entirely pragmatic military grounds that Tito was fighting more effectively against the Germans.

On the other hand, had Soviet leaders foreseen the future defection of Tito and the growing gulf between Russia and a Communist China, they might have been even less outgoing with support during the guerrilla wars that brought these two groups to power.

Then again the policy makers of a national government may decide that they stand to lose rather than gain in their over-all foreign relations should a resistance movement which they have instigated in a neighboring state actually come to power. The Soviets may feel this way about the Iranian Communists today. There is disaffection in Iran, and it is problematical how far the earnest but limited reform and development programs of the government will allay this unrest. The Russians have direct access to and considerable influence with many of the tribes along Iran's northern border. The Russians doubtless wish to stir up all the trouble they can for the government of the Shah and its Western allies. At the same time they probably realize that an unconventional offensive which actually brought the Communists to power in Iran and made the state a subservient Soviet satellite would create violent anti-Soviet feeling throughout the Middle East. This reaction could be so strong as to more than counterbalance any advantages they might gain by possessing Iran. Here then, the Soviet policy may be to keep tensions and uncertainties at a damagingly high level, but to avoid achieving a victorious take-over—a policy both frustrating and dangerous for the Communist leaders in Iran.

In other areas complete victory may have to be avoided for different reasons. In Singapore, for example, Communist influence and organization among the Chinese population is sufficiently strong to assure the ultimate success of a rebellion against the British authorities. Yet the violence and bloodshed which characterized the Communist-led disturbances among the labor unions and student groups in Singapore during the middle fifties has subsided, and the island is enjoying comparative peace and prosperity. This may change rapidly if the Communists see a serious threat in the establishment of a Malayasian state encompassing Singapore, Malaya, British North Borneo, Brunei, and Sarawak, but the reasons for the present tranquillity are fairly clear. Singapore can exist only as a port and entrepôt for the Far Eastern trade of the free world. If the Communists were to take the colony over, and that trade sought other channels, they would find themselves possessed of a depressed and stagnant city with insoluable economic problems.

Thus we see in Singapore a paradoxical situation. The same Communist leaders who rant against the evils of colonialism have no choice but to protect and support the system they avowedly detest, for a victory over it would be disastrous to them.

In some measure the same circumstances apply to the Crown Colony of Hong Kong. A Communist Chinese-sponsored campaign of assassinations, sabotage, civil disorder, and economic embargo would unquestionably make the colony unprofitable and ultimately untenable for the British, but the greater loser in such a Communist victory would be the Communist Chinese themselves, for Hong Kong is their most important window on the free world and their largest source of foreign currency.

Then too, the leaders of an insurrection may find their outside support being curtailed because of their sponsor's feelings that the opposition is growing too strong, and the rebellion has either become a lost cause or that the risks of continuing and raising the level of support are becoming more than the possible gains warrant. We have seen that the cause of the Greek insurgents was made almost hopeless by Tito's defection and the closing of the Yugoslav border. Shortly afterwards the level of support across the Bulgarian border began to decline as well. The Soviet leaders had evidently decided that there was little point in throwing good money after bad, and the Greek Communists were left to their fate.

The withdrawal of support from a promising insurrection from fear that continued assistance may produce escalation into a conventional or general war involving the sponsor has to be looked at as a theoretical possibility, for there are no examples from recent history of such a change of policy taking place for this reason. The strong American position, amounting to a virtual ultimatum, which forced the Soviets to abandon their expansion into Iran in 1946 comes close to illustrating a successful use of this sort of pressure, but the American demand was for the withdrawal of Russian conventional military forces, and the temporary collapse of Communist unconventional efforts followed as an aftermath of that withdrawal.

There is no question that the guerrilla conflicts in which both the rebels and the threatened government receive extensive help from antagonistic larger powers carry within them the seeds of larger conflict, for they can become, in effect, limited wars by proxy. But, as we have seen, unconventional aggression is less susceptible to uncontrolled escalation than any other form of attack. The chief value of the American landings in Lebanon in 1958 and in Thailand in 1962 was that they served as unmistakable indications of intent. They did not put a stop to unconventional aggression; they merely set out the limits within which the struggle was to be fought. They did not in themselves threaten Communist states, for the forces involved were not strong enough or suitably deployed to constitute a threat. Rather, they created trip wires, in much the same way as do the NATO forces in Europe, against which it was patently unsafe for the Communists to press conventional attack, either directly or through satellites.

The last fifteen years have demonstrated that threats of massive retaliation against unconventional aggression are highly ineffective. Their primary weakness is that they are implausible and occasionally downright incredible. Their secondary weakness is that they constitute a purely military response, and a distant one at that, to a localized political danger. Threats of military opposition to the supporters of insurgent aggression must be realistic. If the threatened action does not appear feasible, the threat itself becomes unbelievable, and is better left unspoken. Nations supporting rebellions within the territories of their neighbors are not likely to be deterred by assertions of the victim's friends that they will set the world on fire if the aggression does not stop.

The Communists have demonstrated that the assets which must be invested in supporting an insurrection are not only small, but quite separate from those required to maintain a conventional national military force. Except for small amounts of infantry weapons, communications equipment, and occasional military airlift, the support of guerrillas in a neighboring country calls for different talents and assets than the support of regular troops. Hence, the nation threatened by guerrilla rebels cannot count on reducing their foreign support by mounting raids or sustained attacks against the regular military forces of the unfriendly neighbor who is inciting and nourishing the rebellion.

Until the latter part of stage three of Mao's scenario for revolution, when the rebels are ready and able to work and fight as conventional troops, the guerrillas of an insurgent force and the military units of the nation which is supporting their operations have to be treated as wholly separate entities, related only through the political leadership which sets the strategy and objectives of both.

In today's world, therefore, the outside power which foments and then nourishes a revolution can operate with remarkable freedom, for it has only two possessions of varying importance at stake in the conflict.

One of these is the reputation and prestige which the nation may enjoy with other interested nations. We have seen that under some circumstances success in the venture may damage rather than augment intangible values such as trust and confidence, but in most cases obvious failure is far more serious. We have also seen, however, that the Communists have developed a peculiar immunity to this sort of damage. Encouraging wars of "liberation" is their avowed and much-publicized intention, and this open acknowledgment of what the free world can only consider flagrant moral turpitude draws off much of the shock, if not the sting, of their expected efforts to put the policy into effect. They have now reached a point where a violent but unsuccessful effort to overthrow a free government is viewed less as a scandalous repudiation of international mores than as a slightly lowered batting average in a continuing series of rough games. As we shall see, the major powers of the West are in a distinctly different situation.

The other asset which a supporting state commits to an insurrection in a neighbor's territory is not, properly speaking, a possession, for it is the group of indigenous leaders, friendly to the supporting state, who organize, manage, and fight the battle. The Communist Party has been badly battered in those countries where its efforts at violent insurrection have failed, but many of the parties have shown an almost Phoenix-like ability to resurrect themselves from the ashes of defeat. Furthermore, the dedication of the newcomers seems little if at all diminished from that of the lost members. This revival is a curious and disturbing thing, but in a number of instances, the apparent reasons for it are all too clear. Grievances, either the old ones or ones of comparable intensity, remain unsolved and unredressed by the government. Commendable efforts to broaden the base of democratic government during periods of great social change permit opposition groups to form which are both unacquainted and unconcerned with democratic principles. Communists originate many of these groups and manage to gain control of others. The unwearying organs of Communist propaganda continue to pour forth the alluring line that Communism has the answer to all the frustrations and disappointments of normal economic development, and inevitably some men come to believe them and join in the task of convincing others. Thus the Communist parties restore themselves.

But one element cannot be restored or quickly re-created. That is the competence, cohesion, discipline, and professional conspiratorial leadership which was lost when the Party was defeated and its members killed, captured, or driven abroad. These qualities only develop through long training and experience, and the number of potential leaders in any group is always limited. History can show many examples of armies being hardened and improved by initial defeats, but this can only happen when enough men survive the defeat to preserve the form and semblance of an army, when these men retain their will to fight, and when they have the intelligence and imagination to learn from their failures. The remnants of a smashed rebellion can rarely meet these requirements. Furthermore, the bruised and bleeding population, having suffered one war in their midst, can rarely be aroused to support another until its wounds are healed and its memory dulled. Certainly this last has proved to be the case in Spain. Franco's regime is not popular with large segments of the people, but the remembered miseries of the Civil War make this generation most reluctant to back an effort to eject him by force of arms.

Therefore, a government which decides to incite and support an insurrection in another nation must realize that, while competent revolutionaries have to be highly expendable, they are not easily replaced by equally able men who can hope to operate in an equally favorable environment.

XI

Foreign Support of Insurrection: Behind the Curtains

Most Americans feel an increasing concern at the continuing series of Communist-inspired and -supported insurrections. Mixed with this is a growing sense of frustration at the Communists' demonstrated ability to stir up this type of trouble for their opponents and the free world's painfully obvious inability to do the same thing to them.

While there is comfort in the fact that no nation has brought a Communist regime to power through a free election, it is equally true that no nation where a Communist government has been firmly established has ever renounced its own brand of Communism and returned wholeheartedly to the free world. The cracks and breaks in the monolith of international Communism have appeared as schisms within the structure, the full depth and effect of which few Western observers can estimate. Mao's China, Tito's Yugoslavia, Gomulka's Poland, and Castro's Cuba are all following their own distinctive versions of the faith, but the fact remains that none of these governments has been overthrown or replaced by a non-Communist structure.

This tends to surprise Americans, for despite the rigid censorship of these police states we know that the level of popular discontent in many of them is at least as high as in any states of the non-Communist world, with the possible exception of South Africa.

The free world is clearly on the defensive in unconventional wars, and there is no reliable indication that this situation will change in the foreseeable future. The failure to get counter-offensives underway is certainly not for want of hoping and wishful thinking by Americans and their political representatives. By the early fifties our bewilderment at the Communists' successes was enough to persuade many Americans that only black treason could explain our failure to destroy Communism. The truly extraordinary conceits that were epidemic at the height of the McCarthy period are now merely endemic with a small minority, but some of the concepts which guided our policies in those days are worth reconsidering as possible keys to our continuing difficulties in waging offensive unconventional war.

In the campaign year of 1952, the foreign policy which had come to be known by the much oversimplified term "containment" was denounced as self-defeating, and John Foster Dulles gave the impression that he felt the architects of the containment policy, Secretary of State Dean Acheson and his planning chief, George Kennan (now Ambassador to Yugoslavia) were not only mistaken but somehow immoral to have adopted such an approach to foreign affairs. The policy of liberation which Mr. Dulles proclaimed as the successor to containment had great emotional appeal to many Americans, although it was never made clear how the alluring rewards of liberation were actually to be achieved. During the next years the heightened emphasis on a military doctrine of massive retaliation made it clear to all that we lacked the means to enforce liberation by any means short of a general holocaust, and soon the dreams of easy liberation faded away completely.

In retrospect, it seems that when Mr. Dulles was arguing the feasibility of liberation he was considering not so much the physical strengths and weaknesses of the Communist powers as what he viewed as the cynical immorality of their leaders and their system. This, he felt, must make the whole structure intrinsically unsound. He thus struck a sympathetic chord in many of his countrymen, for moral issues, however conceived and presented, have always been profoundly important to Americans. As an American, I feel deeply that this is a trait we can and should be proud of, but too often it has led to a flat conviction that moral right must ultimately triumph. The Germanic Götterdämmerung has no place in American folklore. While Americans can and do show remarkable energy in times of open war, we slip at other times into a dangerous belief that somehow human dignity and freedom will prevail largely through their own inherent virtue and less through the struggle and sacrifice men make to maintain them. This assumption has clouded American thinking on the forces actually needed to oppose or overthrow a Communist government. God may not, as Voltaire asserted, be on the side of the big battalions, but it is too often forgotten that He has consistently seemed to help those who help themselves.

American uncertainties on the physical and moral demands of unconventional war have led us into some peculiar situations, probably the most spectacular of which was the woebegone invasion of Cuba in the spring of 1961. Feeling that human dignity and freedom needed a helping hand, the United States attempted both to strike a blow and to stay in the background while doing so. In the confusion that accompanied this bit of contortion, the blow proved wholly ineffective and achieved worldwide notoriety.

That operation was not an unconventional offensive in the sense that we are using the word. The invaders were trained and equipped to fight as regular soldiers. Unlike most insurgents who build the political base first and move forward to military action by slow degrees as their strength permits, the Cuban invaders sought an initial military victory, to be followed up by an accelerating political and military campaign, in which the landing force would be re-enforced by members of the population turning against the Castro regime.

The Bay of Pigs attack was certainly unconventional in the

sense that it was a highly unorthodox military effort, and the reasons for its failure will be acrimoniously argued for years to come. It is worthwhile, therefore, to look briefly at the wholly different outcome of what is perhaps the closest modern historical parallel to the Cuban invasion. That occurred in 1860 when Garibaldi and his one thousand fellow revolutionaries scrambled ashore from two transports at Marsala, Sicily, to raise the island in revolt against a Neapolitan garrison of over twenty thousand regular troops. Garibaldi won his first and critical battle against a detachment of these soldiers a few days later at Calatafimi, and thereafter, although the military odds continued fantastically against him, he had the active and wholehearted support of virtually the entire population. A month later Garibaldi had established himself in the Neapolitan capital at Palermo, the garrison had surrendered, and he had won the most extraordinary victory of his thoroughly extraordinary career.

Some fairly obvious factors made this exploit vastly different from the recent Cuban effort. First, Garibaldi was the celebrated, brilliant, and compelling leader of a highly popular cause. There is no indication that the leaders of the Cuban invasion had comparable personal or political magnetism. Then too, the Neapolitan regime in Sicily was both cordially hated and grossly inefficient. Certainly Castro was not universally loved in 1961, but his forces were respected and well led, and his government reacted to the invasion threat with energy and decision. The Neapolitan regime in Sicily seems to have more closely resembled that of Batista in Cuba. Finally, there is the matter of outside support for the invaders. The British historian G. M. Trevelyan reminds his readers of Britain's correct and neutral position,[1] but the record makes this claim a little dubious.

Sir James Hudson, the British consul at Turin, was privy to

[1] *Garibaldi and the Thousand.* London: Longmans, Green & Company, 1909.

and sympathetic with the plans for the invasion. When Garibaldi's transports arrived at Marsala, they found, by strange coincidence, two British warships anchored off the harbor mouth. A small Neapolitan squadron arrived shortly afterwards during a critical stage in the landing, and its commander was startled to learn that the two British captains were ashore in the harbor area. Understandably, he did not open fire in that direction while lying himself under the guns of the British ships. By the time the two Englishmen were rowed out to assure him of their neutrality, the bulk of Garibaldi's men were ashore, and in the ineffective firing which ensued only one of the rebels was wounded. Later in the campaign, when his forces were in the hills, Garibaldi's camp was visited by British officers who conveniently chose that time and place to go sightseeing on the strife-torn island. Through these men he dispatched his letters to Genoa and Turin. It should be noted that some Frenchmen and two American naval officers also visited Garibaldi's headquarters. For a rebel whose hope of success theoretically lay in stealth and surprise, he seems to have entertained foreign guests rather freely. During the campaign a squadron of the Royal Navy lay off the harbor of Palermo. When Garibaldi's men had forced their way into the center of the capital and the Neapolitan leaders sought to arrange a cease-fire, the negotiations were held in the British admiral's cabin. A British naval officer who was sent ashore into the barricaded and bullet-swept streets, acted as go-between in putting a stop to the fighting, and the final surrender of the Palermo garrison was signed on board the British flagship. Later, while the defeated garrison was being evacuated, the Royal Navy ships conducted gunnery practice outside the harbor mouth—a display that must have clearly demonstrated to the Neapolitans the folly of any attempt to renew hostilities with their exhausted and outnumbered conquerors. Trevelyan's protestations to the contrary, his own chronicle of the events makes it clear that Garibaldi received significant foreign support.

Today's military technology makes a small invasion of the Marsala type even more of a forlorn hope than it was a century ago. Unless the invaders have overwhelming air power to support them or heavy fire support from accompanying ships or both, the power of the defenders' weapons is likely to overwhelm them before they can bring comparable strength to bear.

A prompt and widespread rising by the populace might conceivably paralyze the government and make the military defense ineffective, but the possibility is a hypothetical one. We have been reminded once more in Cuba that it takes either the desperation of despair, as shown in the Warsaw ghetto, or the brightest certainty of victory, as seen in pre-liberation Paris, to make civilians hurl themselves at well-armed troops.

And so there are few ways in which unconventional offensives á la Garibaldi can today be carried through to national victory. Where there is dissension among the military forces, *coups d'é-tat* are possible, but the carefully planned and conducted insurrection which combines political and military activity along the lines we now generally associate with Communist-led movements seems in most cases to hold out the best chance of success. It is the feasibility and the rights and wrongs of our sponsoring such operations that we must consider here.

The arguments which favor a policy of supporting rebellions within the Communist world are persuasive. Westerners, and particularly Americans, are emotionally ill-suited to fighting an extended defensive war. We have seen the awful cost in human misery and treasure which the Communist insurrections have imposed on unaggressive free nations, and there is an appealing elemental justice in the idea of turning the aggressor's own weapons back against him. The restive state of many of the Communist-dominated populations and the evident splits among their national leaders argue that some of the nations behind the curtains are ripe for insurrection and successful revolution. Furthermore, there is the chance that even if such insurrections did not overthrow the government, they might deter continued or future unconventional aggression against the free world.

The arguments against the United States instigating insurgency in Communist states have considerably less emotional appeal, but they may possess more cold logic and validity.

Through most of America's history she has, in theory, supported the doctrine of non-intervention in the internal affairs of other countries. The United States has a far higher reputation for honorable and open dealings in her foreign affairs than do any of the Communist states. This reputation was tarnished somewhat by the Cuban adventure of 1961, but it remains an important consideration in the way we conduct our national business. Indeed, even though this doctrine is avowedly violated by the Communists, it is difficult to see how America could openly abandon or modify it without sacrificing much of the genuine respect in which she is held throughout the world, thus paying a stiff price for an increased freedom of action which might actually work to her disadvantage. We have seen that the national Communist parties are uniquely effective instruments for offensives of this sort. The West certainly does not possess an equivalent, and it is problematical at best whether a comparably effective structure could be created behind the Iron and Bamboo Curtains during this generation.

In fact, quite aside from the direct advantages of our maintaining an overt policy of non-intervention, we may be making a virtue of necessity in doing so. There are far-reaching differences in the ways the free nations and the Communists have to approach this sort of work. Since the machinery of a Communist police state is designed to operate without the active support or approval of its subjects, latent and potential unrest is expected and assumed. Confident communication between individuals, without which conspiracy is virtually impossible, is difficult in an atmosphere in which even the school children are used as informers, and the discussion or organization of any opposition movement to the government is a covert and highly dangerous activity. While a rebellious movement must expand if it is ever to be effective as a popular force, the dangers of discovery, betrayal, and suppression increase with every additional recruit. The Communist leaders are certainly not the only ones to place grievous restraints on human freedoms, but in few parts of the free world are the controls anywhere near as pervasive and effective as in the lands behind the curtains.

Then too, the reaction of Communist and Western governments to internal threats by insurrection differ sharply. In South Africa, where the governmental structure is openly patterned to benefit a small minority by exploiting the great majority, violent suppression of dissidents is accepted as logical, but free world governments generally agree that it is better policy to win back disgruntled citizens than to decimate them. Not so the Communists. We have already looked at the Budapest experience as illustrative of what open rebellions are up against in Communist areas.

The Communist planner looking toward an unconventional attack on a free nation knows that he controls in large measure the bloodshed and destruction his offensive will cause. He also knows that the greatest threat to his effort is that the battered government may so repair and improve its position with its own people that it will regain their support and thus pull the rebels' political teeth.

The American or other free world planner considering a comparable offensive into Communist areas faces a very different picture. He knows that his offensive will evoke a ruthless repressive campaign in any areas which give support to the insurrection. This he cannot control and, win or lose, there is bound to be widespread bloodshed and suffering throughout the region he is seeking to liberate. Where the Communist authorities have massive police and military force available to them, they are prone to use it, without much consideration as to the guilt or innocence of the victims. Mao's three-stage scenario of revolution is of limited value under these circumstances. The second or guerrilla stage has to be truncated, for the rebels must be able militarily to defend their popular base among the people soon after the rebellion becomes active. Otherwise that base may well be lost, together with a significant proportion of the population itself.

There are also significant differences in the security problems facing a Communist or a Western sponsor of revolution. The planning and organization of an insurrection against a reasonably alert neighboring government has to be done discreetly if the uprising is to have the best chance of success. In a Communist state, where communications and information media are closely controlled, and travel restrictions are considered more the rule than the exception, the government can assemble, train, care for, and move large numbers of foreign personnel without attracting undue attention. As we saw during the Cuban invasion, activities of this kind are far more complicated in an open society with an energetic free press and an instinctive popular curiosity about anything out of the ordinary.

Americans face a further difficulty in planning and supporting unconventional offensives into Communist areas—a difficulty which we are understandably reluctant to acknowledge. This is the simple fact that it is often hard to set out specific positive political objectives for anti-Communist insurgents.

Communism is repugnant to those who have had a chance to enjoy the benefits of a working democracy. It may not appear this way, however, to a man who only knows about Communism what Communists have told him, who sees it identified with many of his own immediate aspirations, and who is already sorely disenchanted with the political situation he sees in his own country. To such a man, setting up a Communist system may seem a worthy, concrete, and positive goal. If he does join a Communist-led insurrection, his indoctrination will emphasize the Party's active purpose and determination to achieve positive goals which he can understand and support, and it will be drummed into him that his leaders are strong men who know where they are going.

The West has had difficulty in presenting equally positive goals to potential insurgents in Communist-controlled lands. Freedom is a stirring call which has moved men to action from time immemorial, but unfortunately it is abstract, meaning different things to different men, and essentially negative in its application, in that it has meaning only in being freedom from something. It is natural and easy to be anti-Communist, particularly for men who have lived and suffered under Communist rule, but determining an agreed alternative which is compelling enough to lead men to fight and die is far harder.

The difficulty in setting out positive goals has occurred in many revolutions of history. The terror that followed the fall of the monarchy in the French Revolution, the civil war that erupted in Ireland after the British withdrawal, and the turmoil in Russia after the abdication of the last Czar all illustrate the difficulty of successfully carrying through a rebellion into a stable government based even remotely on democratic principles.

When we consider the possibilities of liberating Communist territories by supporting indigenous insurrections we tend to founder on the problems of what can or may come after initial successes. No revolution is complete which merely creates the chaos of a political vacuum. One of the many hideous features of Communist rule is the systematic care with which all potential anti-Communist leadership is rooted out and destroyed, and at the same time, there are few instances in which the leaders who antedated the Communists will be welcomed back to power. The Dalai Lama and his attendant Tibetans in Indian exile could almost certainly go back to Tibet should Communist Chinese rule be overthrown, and up to a decade ago some of the political leaders in the countries of Eastern Europe might have returned to authority after a liberation, but when men have been exiles for many years or carry the stigma for the weaknesses or defeats which led to their ouster, they are not likely to regain popular support. Occasionally when a leader has been expelled by the forceful action of a special group in the national society, as was the case with Perón and the Argentine Army, he may, for better or worse, retain a popular following over the years, but this is exceptional. Castro, for example, may well become increasingly unpopular with his Cuban subjects, but he is not likely to be overthrown in favor of Batista. As the Castro regime weakens, one of its strongest remaining assets may well be the bickering factionalism among the Cuban refugee leaders and the uncertainties of their standing with possible rebellious elements within the island. On the other side of the world it is becoming increasingly evident that the Chinese people are desperately anxious to be done with their Communist masters, but this is no evidence of eagerness to put Chiang Kai-shek back in the saddle.

Then too, the overthrow of some Communist regimes might result in almost more trouble for the West than their continued existence. Albania would almost certainly be a case of this sort. Geographically separated and ideologically alienated from the USSR, the position of the Communist regime in that impoverished country is hardly a strong one. But almost twenty years of Communist rule have effectively destroyed any coherent internal political opposition and outdated the claims of old emigré groups. In the past, Yugoslavia, Greece, and Italy have all layed claim to part or all of Albania, and should the country be plunged into total confusion by the collapse of the government, their latent claims would inevitably take on new life and emotional heat. It is hard to think of a more effective way to disrupt the southern flank of NATO and to wreck Tito's tenuous ties with the West than to have Albanian real estate thrown up for grabs. Indeed, the great powers of the West may conclude that they have an interest in preserving the safety of this nasty little government.

Finally, we must consider the possible consequences to the

West of encouraging risings and conspiracies within the Communist states for their nuisance or deterrent value without providing the means to push them through to full victory. Even though the disaffected peoples of the Communist states are not trained cadres, there is little question that some of them would become insurgents if encouraged to do so and given a reasonable hope of success. They would certainly cause their masters grave inconvenience if they did, but they would have little chance of success, or even survival, without direct and probably extensive aid from the outside. It is wholly alien to our principles and traditions to so exploit the desperation of brave and hopeful men, so we can rule out any policy of inciting foredoomed insurrections in the hope that they may ease pressure on us elsewhere.

If, at the same time, we reject a policy of encouraging insurgency and then supporting the resultant rebellions through to success regardless of the costs, political complications, and dangers of escalated conflict that may be involved, then we had best reject all policies or programs which call for initiating or furthering unconventional offensives in the territory of other nations.

XII

Foreign Support in Counterinsurgency

We have already examined some of the tasks and problems which confront the government of a nation under internal attack by insurrection. Hence, we have touched indirectly on the government's relationship with a stronger outside power that comes to its assistance in fighting off the attack. Still, there are a number of aspects in this relationship which need to be looked at from the viewpoint of the outside friend and ally. This is particularly important for Americans to consider, for in many parts of the world the United States is playing a complicated role which combines being friend, protector, benefactor, teacher, and nurse to smaller countries threatened by or already in serious trouble.

Relationships between friendly or allied nations are never wholly smooth and serene. Complete concord and agreement is patently impossible between disparate blocs of millions of people with different cultures, different traditions, different political systems and who, in many cases, are separated by many thousands of miles. All alliances, back to those of the Greek city-states and probably long before them, have been weakened in some measure by rivalries and misunderstandings among the members, and these difficulties have been increased when linguistic, racial, or religious gulfs have had to be bridged.

America's relationships with the nations she is helping in their fight against unconventional aggression are subject to these ills as well as to others which tend to infect a partnership one member of which is vastly more powerful and secure than the other. The weak tend to distrust and fear the strong, the strong may become impatient with and patronize the weak. These frictions are perhaps incurable in any international effort at cooperation in a difficult task, but they must be remembered, accepted, and kept to a minimum.

Potentially more damaging are the difficulties and frictions which develop from differences in the estimates the two governments make of the nature and urgency of the threat facing them and in the long-term policy objectives of each state. Obviously, both nations are primarily concerned with protecting and furthering their own national security. In America's view the great danger in violent insurrections is that Communist power will move into the vacuum left by the collapse of an existing government. It follows that America's purpose in aiding such a government is to so strengthen it that it can make the difficult changes and advances involved in modernization without breaking down. We must see, as Walt W. Rostow put it, "that this revolutionary process of modernization shall be permitted to go forward in independence, with increasing degrees of human freedom."[1]

The rationale is a simple one. United States security will not be threatened by politically stable and independent states, peacefully developing their own economies within the free world community. It is basic to American political philosophy that such states can and will provide their citizens with the greatest opportunity for the pursuit of happiness and that with growing strength and stability they will finally be able to protect themselves against the unconventional "wars of national liberation" which are now the prime Communist strategy of aggression. The American government is committed to seeking a system of worldwide collective security through the United Nations and it be-

[1] Address to the graduating class at the U. S. Army Special Warfare School, Fort Bragg, N.C., June 28, 1961.

lieves that America's own safety increases with the appearance of new stable, peaceful, potentially prosperous and increasingly democratic states.

This, broadly stated, is the principle of American policy as it appears today. The sad but inevitable difficulty is that the principle loses some of its pristine simplicity and clarity in practical application.

The governmental leaders of the countries America is helping are just as concerned about their security and survival as Americans are about their own, but in many of the newer or less-developed states the concept of the nation is neither well understood nor highly regarded. The Congo experience has given us a violent and vivid example of the lively loyalties that tribalism and regionalism can still evoke. At the same time, in many of the older states the leaders' primary concept of security is built more around the culture, the class, the economic grouping, or even the individual than around the nation as a whole.

In countries where Communist-inspired rebellion is a threat but not yet a reality, such leaders are likely to consider the United States concern for their well-being and progress as downright quixotic, occasionally irritating, but definitely useful. As we have seen in Chapter Eight, these men feel that they know their country and the dangers that may beset it far better than outsiders. They may prefer to ignore the potentially lethal shortcomings of their own administration which make them vulnerable to subversion and revolt, and they definitely feel that it is no business of the Americans to tell them their supposed failings. The reaction of some Latin Americans to the much-vaunted Alliance for Progress provides a case in point here. Still, United States concern is often accompanied by United States bounty, both military and economic, and this tends to put a different light on things. The government leaders may feel that the American interest in Communism is somewhat obsessive and our recommendations for change and reform are unnecessary and almost in bad taste, but they usually decide that awkward audiences with the American ambassador and with roving American congressmen is an acceptable price to pay for much-wanted and often desperately needed aid.

When a cooperative effort gets under way, the government leaders push the programs they wish or feel are necessary, and the United States representatives assist in these and usually press for other and more extensive ones. Thus is consumated a political marriage of a sort which is likely to benefit both parties, but which can have some wholly unintended consequences. The knowledge that American prestige and strength are now committed to assist them eases the problems of the threatened nation's leaders, and it is only human that they seek to use this advantage for their own purposes. As we have seen there is a temptation to paint all political opposition to them as Communist-influenced or -led. The confidence inspired by strong American backing also may tempt the leaders to defer the very reforms which the American aid was intended to facilitate, the reasoning being that the regime is now so firmly entrenched and backed that these inconvenient and distasteful changes are no longer necessary. This appears to have been the case in China during the immediate postwar years.

Then too, American aid that is intended to further modernization and to reduce the threat of Communist expansion may increase antagonisms and regional rivalries which have little or nothing to do with Communism or direct American interests. For example, there was considerable concern voiced in India when Pakistan joined the Southeast Asia Treaty Organization. Relations between the two countries had been strained by religious differences and by the Kashmir controversy and, despite the fact that the wording of the treaty and all public statements made by its signers emphasized that it was directed solely against Communist expansion, the Indians professed to see something sinister in the new link.

If Communist-inspired insurrection has already broken out in a nation receiving United States assistance, the American relationship with its government is subject to many of the same strains, but they take on a new intensity and urgency. The task becomes one of curing rather than preventing a disease, and the time factor becomes critical. The level of assistance provided increases, and almost inevitably, the emphasis shifts heavily to the military end of the scale, with considerations of long-term development giving way to the immediate demands of the fighting. This very shift can be the subject of additional differences between the national leaders and their foreign benefactors. The former naturally see themselves involved in a struggle for personal survival, and tend to forget whatever they may have previously recognized as their own contributions to the national weakness. The Americans, being more detached and not immediately threatened, urge maintaining and if possible stepping up the long-term development and reform measures, many of which the national leaders felt all along to be of dubious value.

Still, the demands of the hour make it clear that the military effort must be increased, and additional aid is provided. American military personnel are dispatched to the area, and if the situation demands, they take an increasingly active part in the operations. During the Huk insurrection in the Philippines, American military materiel, backed up by a relatively small number of American advisers, was all the outside military aid that a highly competent national government needed to defeat the Communist-led insurrection.

In South Vietnam the situation has proved to be infinitely more complicated and difficult. There it became clear that material aid and discreet military guidance would not be enough to stave off disaster. Thereafter, the pattern of the American buildup was a logical one. The United States Government, having decided that its own national security was deeply involved and its prestige committed, first sent in additional advisers on counterguerrilla operations and then specialist troop units to provide logistic and training support for the Vietnamese forces. It was obvious from the day these men arrived that no clear line could be drawn between support and combat duties. The men were shot at, casualties were sustained, and the United States was soon avowedly engaged in an open military effort to suppress the insurrection, an effort now closely linked to the massive economic aid effort that has continued since South Vietnam became an independent state.

At this stage we come up firmly against the central dilemma which inevitably confronts the foreign ally and protector in situations of this sort. The problem was anticipated, for the United Nations encountered it a decade ago while fighting a different sort of war in Korea. The simple fact is that when one nation directly and openly undertakes the military defense of a weaker state against attack, particularly unconventional attack, the helping nation involves itself in far more than mere military defense, for the attack is far more than military. With American soldiers committed, America must also concern itself directly with the political and social weaknesses which made the nation particularly vulnerable in the first place and which will prevent or retard its winning through to political stability.

No campaign which directly determines the fate of a nation and immediately influences the daily life of all its citizens can be conducted with disparate plans and conflicting objectives, so that a considerable degree of agreement is essential. In the eyes of the world the bigger of the two powers is viewed as largely responsible for the policies and acts of the smaller, so it becomes not only damaging but highly embarrassing when the policies of the two openly diverge.

But in some measure this is happening now in many parts of the world. The United States finds itself linked in varying degrees with many governments whose philosophies and methods of operation are sharply alien to American thinking and whose policies strike many Americans as far from wise. Most of these marriages of convenience have come into being through the American leaders' realization that the dubious friend is almost certainly better than any alternative that might replace him, and their hope that somehow they will be able to persuade him to mend his ways. Nevertheless, it is fatuous to assume that even those governments with which the United States has cooperated most closely will willingly accommodate by acting against what its leaders feel to be their national or personal best interest.

In the course of the Korean War it became clear that the government of South Korea would violently oppose any end to the hostilities before the United Nations forces had conquered and occupied the whole length of the peninsula. Forces representing many of the great nations of the free world were deeply engaged, and the South Korean leaders saw that a continuation of the fighting was their best chance of unifying the entire country. This last was their primary objective. It was of little or no concern to these men that the state they governed had been redeemed, that the war had thereafter become intensely unpopular with their allies and supporters, and that a drive to the north would be bloody, costly, and a distinct threat to the over-all peace of the world. The Rhee government's opposition to a settlement reached its peak in June 1953 when, in violation of the tentative truce agreement, the South Koreans released the North Korean prisoners who were in their custody, thereby delaying the armistice for another month. Naturally the Americans resented this as an irresponsible breach of faith by an ally. This it certainly was, but viewed in terms of the rigid, hardly realistic, and highly regional objectives of the leaders of a small nation who felt that in their own land they were being overborne by outside influence, it at least becomes partially understandable. Rhee's reactions to the events around him were extreme and illogical, but they illustrate the sort of thing that is likely to arise in different forms elsewhere.

America's leaders have stated repeatedly and sincerely that the United States does not seek satellites, but her position in the free world and the nature of the Communist threat forces her constantly to urge smaller states into positions and policies of her choice. At best this process is patronizing; at worst it can lead to forms of pressure and coercion which appear to belie America's honest desire to encourage the growth of free and independent nations.

The delicacy of this process and the damage that can result from vagueness in determining American policies in these matters or ineptitude in carrying them out make it critically important that the nation's leaders be fully aware of the implications of their actions and the consequences that may be expected to flow from them. Some tough decisions have to be considered and made in determining the appropriate attitude and actions of the United States toward a smaller nation threatened by subversion and insurrection.

First is the question of whether America's own national interest firmly demands that help be given to the threatened state in defending its independence and in furthering its modernization and development. Through formal alliances or by the granting of economic and military aid, the United States has given clear notice of its intent to assist a large number of governments in their struggle toward progress and stability. Each instance in which additional action is urged must be carefully considered on its own merits if America is not to overextend her protective and supporting arm by providing more aid to more nations than her national security actually requires.

There follows the more complex problem of how best to assure that the government receiving American aid follows a general line of policy that is desirable both from its own viewpoint and that of the United States. There is certainly nothing to be gained by simply standing by while American policies are frustrated and American prestige sapped by leaders who waste or mistakenly exploit the aid provided them.

Inevitably this is a tricky business. Advice, counsel, and cooperation are all acceptable terms and concepts, even when both parties are fully aware of the pressures being exerted, but anything that smacks too openly of coercion or bullying may boomerang politically against the larger nation and cause difficulties not only with the smaller ally but with other nations as well. Still, some method of exerting polite but effective control has to be found. American programs in a number of states amount to heavy commitments, but in some, and at the time of writing South Vietnam is an example, the United States cannot exert sufficient leverage decisively to influence the course of events. This is particularly important in some South American countries and perhaps Iran, where the political, social, and economic frustrations of increasingly powerful elements in the population create a highly promising atmosphere for subversion and hostile exploitation.

The critical point, and one which it is difficult to face, is that when the leaders of a threatened government will not or cannot undertake realistic measures to strengthen the bases of their popular support and to reduce the danger of subversion and insurrection, American interest cannot be served by further supporting them. At that point a highly unpleasant choice has to be made. If a successful insurrection would vitally and immediately threaten United States security, there is really no alternative but to intervene directly, either unilaterally, together with allies, or in support of an international organization. This situation arose in the Congo in the summer of 1960 and led to the UN operation in that country. In the majority of cases the threat will not be so evident or immediate. Then the realistic course will be to cut American losses, both in prestige and materiel, discontinue the aid which is not achieving its purpose, and leave the country to the confusion and unconventional aggression which its leaders have invited.

These, of course, are the alternatives of last resort. Usually the important interests of American security can be protected and furthered by far less drastic steps. In considerable measure Americans' feelings of frustration and uncertainty in regions threatened by this sort of aggression stem from their own failure to size up the realities of the situation correctly or to make the best use of the assets they have available.

In some cases Americans have tended to forget that the endangered government has no real alternative but to follow the general policies urged upon it so long as these policies are made the condition of American aid. Quite rightly the United States has left the administration of much of its aid to the indigenous authorities, seeking only to see that it is applied as effectively as possible to the improvement of the national economy and the furtherance of political stability. Too often American authorities have succumbed to pressure, amounting almost to a fatuous form of blackmail, and allowed the aid to go to further relatively useless or even damaging ends which appealed to the fancy or the ambitions of the local leaders. These pressures have been somewhat like the proverbial threat of the spoiled child that "I will hold my breath until I'm dead, and then you'll be sorry." The leaders present themselves and their cherished projects as the only alternatives of collapse, chaos, and Communist victory. Thus we see heavy artillery and similar military equipment going to nations which have little if any need for it, as in parts of Latin America, unrealistically large armies being maintained at the expense of shaky economies, as in Iran, and well-financed political administrations which stifle initiative and imagination but protect the personal power and prerogatives of the men or man at the top.

This sort of blackmail succeeds and persists because of American failure to think through the probable alternatives to going along with it, and reluctance to do anything that might ruffle superficially smooth short-run relations with the government in question.

On other occasions Americans have felt frustrated and let down by the performance of the threatened government receiving their support, but the fault has lain with their own misunderstanding of that government's problems and limitations. While United States leaders obviously do not expect mutually antagonistic jungle tribes to transform themselves overnight into the states of a Jeffersonian democracy, their expectations of political cohesion and development are sometimes unrealistically high. The American attitude toward the Kingdom of Laos over the past few years is an example here. The diverse peoples of that remote and little-developed area have little or no sense of national unity. Transportation and communications are worse than poor. There is neither effective central government, nor the normal foundations on which political administration is built; such things as a working civil service, a functioning judicial system, and a sound system for tax collection are all woefully lacking. The Laotian national personality or spirit, if such a thing exists, is certainly not well defined and is not capable or conditioned to fight in defense of its own integrity. It has been evident for some time that the task of the leaders in Laos is not to reform existing weaknesses and inequities in the system, but rather to build a system pretty much from the ground up. This is clearly going to take considerable time and doing. Instead of being bewildered at Laos' inability and apparent lack of interest in defending itself, the United States should have realized that Laos could not be built in a day or in five years and should have set its expectations accordingly.

In other instances American frustration and disappointment stem from a confusion of judgment between those moves by a threatened government that are essential to U.S. national security and those that would be gratifying and heartwarming but not vitally important. This uncertainty crops up in a number of different forms and is difficult to resolve, as the problems usually center on emotion-charged intangibles such as national dignity, *amour-propre,* and hurt feelings.

One instance of this confusion is the matter of American aid to left-wing governments, a perennial hot potato in the Congress and the press. Nothing would please the Soviet leaders more than to see the Tito government of Yugoslavia so weakened that it would be vulnerable to subversion and unconventional aggression. Knowing this and realizing that a Russian-dominated Yugoslavia would critically weaken the southern flank of NATO, the United States has granted Tito substantial aid to preserve and strengthen his regime. These grants have never signified or symbolized American approval of his system of government. Yugoslavia is still a police state with at least outwardly good relations with the Soviets and, while there are encouraging indications of increasing freedom of action for the individual citizen, no serious observer has argued to the contrary.

Instead, American aid has been justified on the pragmatic acceptance of three fairly obvious facts. First, that Tito's government is of positive value to the West both as a physical bloc to Soviet expansion in the Balkans and as a symbol of disunity in the Communist world. Second, that should the present government weaken and fail, the Soviets, working across the contiguous borders of Hungary, Romania, and Bulgaria, would be in a far better position than the West to exploit the ensuing confusion to their own advantage. Third, that the Tito government has demonstrated over some years its ability to govern, that it has moved away from the Soviet orbit of direct control, and now sees Russia as its primary, and indeed almost only, external threat. For these reasons, and because the West can present no plausible and acceptable alternative to Tito's regime, it has seemed wisest to assure that government the means to preserve Yugoslav independence and to develop and evolve in its own fashion.

Against these practical considerations have to be balanced the facts that Tito is an avowed Communist, by his own definition of the term, and that he and his followers seem to delight in criticizing, if not openly biting, the hand that feeds them. These characteristics are irritating and occasionally infuriating to the American leaders who provide Yugoslavia with the aid it needs so badly, but it is another question whether they affect the requirements of American national security.

In other instances the foreign statement or action that disappoints and annoys the American leader and taxpayer may be quite minor, but its very pettiness may magnify the irritation it produces.

Examples of this sort of thing are frequent, and it seems the best solutions are patience and a sense of humor. For instance, in June 1962, the government of South Vietnam solemnly prohibited its people from indulging in the widely practiced recreation of dancing with each other. The move was evidently a rather shotgun approach to suppressing prostitutes working as taxi dancers in Saigon. The American authorities therefore acceded to the Vietnamese order and decreed in turn that there should be no more dancing by United States citizens. Obviously no thinking American wishes to affront the ethical standards of the people among whom he lives and works or to stand in the way of what may be an inept but advisable effort to clean up a wide open town, but the sweeping nature of the order aroused some comment. The subsequent statement by the acting first lady of Vietnam, Mme. Ngo Dinh Nhu, that "if the Americans want to dance, they should go elsewhere,"[2] seems both arrogant and a little silly considering that her nation survives today because of American support and presence. Still this sort of needling does not alter the critical considerations for U.S. national security which have led America to advise and finally to help

[2] *Time* Magazine, June 22, 1962, p. 40.

on the spot in South Vietnam. Only a conclusion that the basic policies and attitudes of that government are actively working against U.S. security interests and defeating U.S. objectives would lead America to reverse her decision to stand by it, and the fact that United States representatives in the area are denied the opportunity to dance with their own countrywomen hardly warrants that conclusion.

There are cases, of course, where the behavior of the leaders of the government the United States is trying to help does become sufficiently irritating and abusive to raise real doubts whether the goals the aid is intended to achieve are worth the steady abrasion on American tempers, nerves, and political relations elsewhere in the world. There is no question that many Americans feel the aid program to India falls into this category today. Prime Minister Nehru's phenomenal sensitivity to any move or statement by an American spokesman which does not appear to support all aspects of Indian policy is vexing to say the least. An example here is his explosive reaction to the remarkably mild motion advanced in the United Nations in 1962 urging a settlement of the Kashmir dispute with Pakistan. This outburst was particularly irritating to American feeling in view of his repeated and outspoken criticism of many aspects of United States policy. The flagrant Indian attack on the tiny Portuguese holding of Goa reduced Nehru's incessant and unctuous protestations of his love of peace to blatantly cynical hypocrisy and complicated America's relations within NATO. Many Westerners find the Indian government harder to live with than the Yugoslav. Tito is at least an avowed Communist with evident and easily comprehended problems. The Indians sometimes appear unpredictable and unabashedly opportunistic.

Nevertheless, Americans have to consider objectively the arguments for continuing the extensive aid now being given to the new and far from secure Indian nation. India is seeking at the same time to modernize and develop her economy and to maintain an advanced form of political democracy. She is the largest Asian state attempting this, and inevitably many of the under-developed nations of the world are comparing for their own purposes the progress she makes with that of the Communist-dominated states. She and the example she is setting are the greatest counterbalance to Communism in the lives and minds of many hundreds of millions of the world's peoples, and as such the West does have a vast interest in seeing that her efforts to achieve economic prosperity and political stability do not fail. The arguments for continuing and perhaps increasing United States aid will become far stronger should the Chinese probing and thrusting on India's northern frontiers grow into a serious attempt at national conquest.

Still, democracies, like the citizens who make them up, have limits to their tempers and do not always act rationally in their own long-term interests. In time Americans may find the be-havior of India's leaders too much to stomach and discontinue aid to that struggling nation. But before that is done, the United States will have to consider the consequences for its own security should India decline into economic breakdown and political confusion. Nehru and company may be difficult to deal with, but the potential alternatives are hardly encouraging.

This raises the obvious question of whether the United States is doing all that it can and should to persuade, influence, and guide the nations threatened with internal difficulties and un-conventional aggression. Unfortunately, the very variety and complexity of the measures this country is taking to assist these states and the structure of the United States Government itself make this a hard matter to evaluate. The American ambassador, with a relatively small immediate staff, coordinates and, in theory at least, directs and controls the activities of a variety of Ameri-cans who represent many government departments and agencies, military and civilian, with distinct but occasionally overlapping functions. Even if all these men are competent, dedicated, and hard-working, it is almost inevitable that discrepancies and even conflicts will emerge among the programs on which they are advising and assisting.

To this cast of relatively permanently placed American players must be added the innumerable birds of passage who flock to and through any exciting trouble spot. Touring congressmen and military and civilian officials on inspection trips interview high officials and usually make public statements, which in turn are reviewed, interpreted, and commented on by nationally syndicated reporters whose own statements sometimes seem to take on a semiofficial quality.

It is little wonder that under these circumstances the leaders of a nation receiving United States aid become confused and occasionally thoroughly irritated at the obvious difficulty of figuring out what all the Americans are up to. Their problem is seldom eased by reports from their own ambassador in Washington, who has the even more frustrating task of figuring out the interrelated responsibilities of the different departments while still, as protocol demands, limiting his direct official contacts to the Department of State.

Orchestrating the over-all American effort so that the whole is greater than the sum of its parts is always a complicated task and at times it appears to be almost an impossible one, but we must never forget that the United States has tremendous assets to dispose and some highly effective instruments of policy to wield.

The traditional limits of conventional diplomacy have been considerably stretched in the years since World War II. The variety and extent of American activities abroad have led to a form of participation in the internal affairs of friendly states which would have profoundly shocked any diplomat of a generation ago. But if he is to be effective, today's American ambassador to a nation threatened with unconventional aggression and aided by the United States must realize that his appropriate sphere of activity is vastly broadened, and he must be ready and able to meet his wider task without losing his objectivity as an observer. From the very start, he has to realize that he is in reality a silent, limited partner in the activities of the government to which he is accredited, and that in the last analysis the leaders of that government need him and all that he can provide them far more than he or the United States Government needs them or the integrity of their nation. These are the harsh realities of the struggle against subversion in the underdeveloped nations. Courtesy, tact, sensitivity, and understanding are all critically important to the ambassador, but so is the appreciation that the traditional niceties of intercourse among nations cannot disguise or satisfy what is in many states a serious need for guidance and leadership.

XIII

International Cooperation in Unconventional War

As we saw in the last chapter, most Americans have come to realize that in the long run their own national security can best be assured by the growth of free and independent nations and that the new and growing states must have help and protection while they are finding their feet. Still America's determination to protect herself and to aid these states during their formative years is only equaled by her determination to reduce her unilateral costs and commitments at the earliest suitable date. The United States has willingly and earnestly assumed what seems to be the mid-century version of the white man's burden, but there is no question that the load chafes the shoulders. No nation enjoys both paying high taxes and seeing its young men in uniform and dispersed to the far ends of the earth, and these trials are made still more irritating by the constant Communist assertions that Americans are wild-eyed galloping militarists and imperialists.

For a number of reasons this chafing is growing increasingly uncomfortable. It is clear that many of the emergent nations have a long way to go before they can achieve political and economic stability, and it follows that for many years to come they will need help if their efforts to modernize themselves are not to break down in disorder and confusion.

It is also becoming clear, as we move further into the nineteen sixties, that the United States alone cannot and should not bear virtually the whole load of helping along the nations of the free world. The results of aid extended over the years have certainly justified the strain on the American economy, but the very success of many of these programs has constantly increased the competition which American industries must face in a gradually more prosperous and productive free world. The truly remarkable recovery which Western Europe has made since the Marshall Plan came into being in 1947 clearly illustrates this. The ability of Europe and Japan to compete with the United States on even or better than even terms in most of the markets of the world is an obvious and in many ways a welcome indicator that the days of sole American responsibility are coming to an end. This burgeoning power, particularly in the Common Market bloc, and the recurrent adverse flows of American gold make it natural that American leaders should cast about with increasing urgency for new sources of help and cooperation. Speaking in September 1962, President Kennedy said "I know that other countries do not expect us to bear indefinitely both the responsibilities of maintaining an international currency and, in addition, a disproportionate share of the costs of defending the free world and fostering social and economic progress in the less developed parts of the world."[1]

The question then becomes one of determining how the industrialized and militarily more powerful nations of the free world can most effectively share the task of advancing and stabilizing the underdeveloped countries now threatened by subversion and rebellion. Roughly parallel but essentially independent national efforts are a possibility. Joint programs worked out through alliances of free states make up another, and there remains the opportunity of working through existing or new in-

[1] Address to the joint session of Governors of the International Bank for Reconstruction and Development and the International Monetary Fund, September 20, 1962.

ternational organizations. There are pros and cons to each
approach, and a mixture of all three is probably the answer.

Certainly many of the Western European states now have
the economic capability to participate, and their interest in the
peaceful and free development of the emergent nations is as
great or greater than our own. However, in some of the states
imperiled by subversion and possible economic collapse, the new
leaders' memories of colonialism and their exaggerated, but natural, desire to demonstrate complete independence from their
old masters tends to inhibit close links with the industrialized
nations that know most about their problems. For example, the
Indonesians are hardly likely to welcome Dutch advice and assistance in managing their affairs for a good many years to come.

In other areas, however, this mood seems to be changing or
wholly different. The leaders of some newly independent peoples realistically appreciate the need to continue beneficial associations. It now appears that Algeria may be a case in point.
The present government there seems to be aware that the country
will be dependent both on close economic ties with France and
on the talents and skills of many French residents for at least a
generation to come. The present indications that many Belgians
will continue to live and work in the new states of Burundi and
Rwanda mark a significant and welcome change from the debacle
that followed independence in the Congo.

The next few years should see a considerable increase of European commercial and official activity in the underdeveloped areas.
The need for new markets and sources of materials, the gradually
lessening venom of the colonial issue, and the growing appreciation of the political importance of the contested areas will all
work toward this end.

There are, however, some definite drawbacks to the bilateral
approach to aid. The motivations of any assisting power may be
wholly unsordid, but they are never above suspicion, and all too
often there is some basis for the suspicion. In addressing the

directors of the International Bank for Reconstruction and Development in September 1962, the retiring president of the Bank, Mr. Eugene R. Black, stated, "My most serious criticism of bilateral aid programs is their susceptibility to political influence, whether overt or otherwise. Even at its best there is always the risk that political influences may misdirect development aid, since they may bring in considerations that are irrelevant to the real needs."

Alliances and regional groupings of states may prove to be effective in averting subversion and unconventional aggression while easing the strains of modernization. The South East Asia Treaty Organization and the Central Treaty Organization of the Middle East do not hold much promise in this direction, but these are primarily military alliances, designed to meet overt aggression, and it may be possible in the future to modify or expand their terms and purposes. The Alliance for Progress among the nations of the Western Hemisphere is designed and intended, as the name implies, to help the member nations in improving economic and social conditions and thus to remedy or preclude the grievances which lead to subversion and insurrection.

It is too early to foretell how effective this effort will be, but it seems clear that for the next decade at least, the United States will make the major inputs to the alliance, and that for practical purposes it will be a predominantly United States effort to strengthen the security of the hemisphere.

Unfortunately, alliances and regional groupings intended to counter unconventional aggression are subject to all the ills of usual alliances as well as a few of their own. Differences in the specific long-term objectives of the member states prevent them from working in full cooperation and with complete candor. When they are concerning themselves with the internal problems of one of their number, suspicions tend to grow among them that one or another is acting with ulterior motives to gain political or commercial advantage or to shift the power balances in the region. It matters little whether or not these suspicions are justified; the effectiveness of the group drops as they increase. The traditional distrust among many geographic neighbors is still dangerously near the surface and, conversely, lack of mutual knowledge and understanding between allies that are distant from each other, or relatively newly acquainted, tends to produce a distrust that is equally damaging. The concept of international interdependence has a long way to go before these misgivings can be completely allayed.

The formal international organizations of the world, most particularly the United Nations, make up another potentially important instrument for furthering politically stable independent nations and economic growth, but here too there are a good many practical difficulties in actual application.

The virtual universality of membership of the United Nations unescapably hampers its effectiveness in coping with aggression by or against states associated with one of the major power blocs. The UN intervention in Korea was only made possible by Russia's blunder in absenting itself from the meeting of the Security Council which considered the North Korean attack, and it is hardly likely that this sort of mistake will be repeated. We must assume that obtaining UN action to prevent or arrest unconventional aggression will be even more difficult, for by its nature the attack will be far harder to pin down and prove.

Most United Nations interventions in international crises or conflicts have concerned disputes where neither Communist-bloc nor Western interests were primarily or immediately involved, and where it was evidently to the benefit of all the major powers that hostilities be prevented or brought to a stop. The dispatch of a UN observation team to the Kashmir early in the Pakistani and Indian dispute there and the interposition of a UN force in the Gaza Strip between the Israeli and Egyptian armies are both examples of this sort of action.

The UN move into the Congo in 1960 was a virtually unique

instance of intervention by an international body into the affairs
of a single state which was patently unable to protect its own integrity if left unaided. Several cogent lessons for the future
emerged from that operation.

First, such intervention is only possible when a good part of
the Western and Communist blocs and a significant number of
the uncommitted nations all feel that it is in their interest to take
action. Since the Communists have demonstrated again and
again that they view as desirable only those operations which
promise them an opportunity to extend their influence and control, and since a sufficient number of non-Communist states are
determined that this shall not happen, it follows almost automatically that in any intervention in which both blocs participate
they will back opposing indigenous forces or factions, and some
form of civil war is likely to result. In the Congo the Lumumba-
Gizenga drive for power constituted the pro-Communist effort.

Second, the Western bloc within the United Nations, sometimes supported by other free states, can combine to prevent a
Communist expansive effort from succeeding, but the differing
positive objectives of the different nations are likely to create
schisms once the initial threat is out of the way. The feelings
aroused among and within the nations of the West by the United
Nations campaign to put down the secessionist move in Katanga
illustrates this tendency.

The point and purpose of the United Nations move into the
Congo had been to make possible the creation and survival of a
politically and economically viable independent state, and it was
evident from the start that without the wealth and natural resources of Katanga no Congolese state could long hope to survive.

The United States and other Western members of the United
Nations were further impelled by the well-founded fear that
should the Congo dissolve into a sort of tropical and primitive
Balkans, the Soviets might well gain firm control over one of the
residual tribal areas and thus establish a dangerous bridgehead in

central Africa. Nevertheless, the use of internationalized soldiery to assure the needed unity produced some sharp reactions. For a while in the United States contentions as to the relative socialistic tendencies of the Leopoldville and Elizabethville governments blurred the public's recollection of the primary objectives in the original intervention, and the Kennedy administration suffered some heavy partisan criticism for its staunch and continued support of the United Nations command.

The third lesson to be drawn from the Congo experience is related to the second, and is simply that an international organization is bound to suffer from the same difficulties as do its individual members. Properly relating the military, economic, and political aspects of a single campaign against insurrectionary and revolutionary forces is a task that the Western nations have hardly yet mastered on their own. We will only deceive ourselves if we believe that a complex international organization, new to the game and suffering from serious internal divisive strains, can prepare itself quickly to carry a major part of the burden.

To date, the International Bank for Reconstruction and Development, generally known as the World Bank, has been far and away the most effective organization in this field. Loans from the Bank have provided funds for development work in every corner of the globe and, while the United States contributions and participation have been disproportionately large, the Bank does constitute a proven international tool for approaching the economic difficulties which contribute to the breakdown of weak or seriously threatened governments.

The success of the World Bank has been due in large measure to imaginative and scrupulously objective leadership, but the main reason why the organization has been able to function as smoothly as it has is that Yugoslavia is the only Communist state that has joined. Thus the Bank is largely spared the obstructionism which has frequently delayed and hindered the United Nations.

In sum, the United States pre-eminent, if diminishing, position among the nations of the West makes it certain that for the near future she must continue to be the primary source of outside help for states threatened by subversion and unconventional attack. Increasing contributions and investments by other industrialized nations will contribute to the stability and prosperity of the emerging areas, and in special situations these nations may be able to make military moves to prevent the overthrow of threatened governments. Britain, for example, moved swiftly and effectively when Kuwait was threatened by Iraq, but the friendly assets for such moves are not likely to meet the sum of the needs for some time to come. In the meanwhile, American determination to protect and assist a threatened nation will be the best guarantee of its independence and healthy growth.

Once that determination is recognized, other national and international bodies may join effectively in the effort, but Americans must face the expensive fact that for some time to come the initiative will have to be theirs.

XIV

Conclusion

In the previous chapters we have looked at a number of aspects of unconventional warfare as it is being waged today. We have seen that the aggressors in these conflicts mount a complex campaign involving subversion, guerrilla forces, and psychological and economic offensives. The government's defensive or counterinsurgency campaign is even more complicated, involving greater expenses, larger forces, and numerous new political problems both at home and abroad. We have also seen something of the tasks the United States Government must face and the obstacles it must overcome in assisting to counter this form of attack against the weaker states of the free world. The final question that we must consider is how the free nations can best prepare themselves to meet these problems and fight this threat.

Any individual approaching this subject is bound to consider it primarily in terms of the strengths, weaknesses, and attitudes of his own country. Consequently, since this writer is an American, the following pages reflect his views of America's position and problems.

The first, and perhaps the most difficult, requirement is that we as a people understand the nature of these conflicts and adjust our traditional concepts of diplomacy, peace, and war to fit the demands of today's world.

There still exists, of course, the danger of all-out war which has historically hung over societies which are divided into basically competitive, antagonistic, and well-armed camps. To reduce this danger we maintain the thermonuclear weapons systems which make up our strategic forces, while we continue the discouraging but essential negotiations to arrive at some realistic and effective arrangement for controlling and ultimately reducing these forces. But we long ago realized that our very success in these efforts could well result in the Communist leaders shifting their continuing expansionist drives into more limited ranges of force and violence. They have done so, and the result is unconventional warfare as we are seeing it today and will almost certainly see it for many years to come.

The prospect of a series of long, localized, delicate, but demanding low-keyed struggles is certainly not a pleasant one, and it is deeply distasteful to the American national personality. If forced to fight for our security, we like to put our back into it and win a war once and for all. In warfare we have the unconditional victory habit and, luckily, we have usually had the strength and energy to indulge it.

To most Americans, limiting a fight to one locality where our objective is to restore gradually a measure of political order and to encourage economic growth doesn't somehow seem the right way to gain a meaningful victory. There is nothing open and shut about this sort of conflict, and men who rationally realize the danger and folly of intentionally escalating the scale and scope of battle still yearn for a way to get it over with quickly. We tend to feel that there is something slack and a little discreditable in living beside or negotiating with an enemy, immediate or potential, who obviously is very much alive and kicking and obviously eager to hurt us and our friends.

The resulting sense of anger and frustration leads many Americans to feel we are following a "no win" policy, even though they themselves can advance no feasible alternatives. We do not feel that our dead in these struggles have died in vain, but their deaths are not gaining for the country the sort of victory to which we have been accustomed.

Certainly a considerable part of our difficulty in coping with this sort of conflict stems from our long-standing custom of viewing war as a purely military matter. First and foremost there is the task of destroying the enemy. Only then do we begin to consider seriously the necessary repair work that has to follow.

Grant's famous assurance to Lee at Appomattox that the men of the Army of Northern Virginia might keep their horses for the spring plowing was a sensible and wonderfully prompt shift from military to political and economic thinking. Other northern leaders were both slower and more vindictive, and they so troubled General Sherman, not noted for his lenience in war, that he wrote his wife, "I perceive the politicians are determined to drive the confederates into guerrilla bands, a thing more to be feared than open organized war."[1] Had Lincoln lived, the Reconstruction era might have been far different, but it seems clear that Grant and Sherman had a far better appreciation of political realities than did most of their colleagues in Washington.

After World War I the shift from all-out military thinking was rapid indeed. The wave of isolationism in America brought the AEF home well ahead of schedule, and Herbert Hoover's relief operations, which during the war had provided aid to allied civilians, were expanded to encompass virtually all the peoples of a distressed and ravished Europe. When the unconditional surrenders finally ended World War II, the process was repeated on a vastly increased scale. First there was the well-nigh frantic demobilization of the armed forces, and then in 1947 the Marshall Plan was launched, with results familiar to all of us.

The counterinsurgency operations that are necessary to defeat unconventional aggression disrupt this tidy and traditional se-

---

[1] *Home Letters of General Sherman* (edited by M. A. De Wolfe Howe). New York: Charles Scribner's Sons, 1909, p. 350.

quence of events. From the start we are fighting to build up a nation, not to defeat one, and we find this sort of war confusing.

The lack of a tidy, easily discernible objective raises other doubts in the minds of many Americans when they consider the nature and the demands of counterinsurgency operations. As we have already noted, the United States was conceived in subversion and born in insurrection, and we tend to be a little uncomfortable at the possibility that we may be interfering in roughly comparable processes elsewhere. Some of the governments we are supporting and protecting fall far short of being democracies by any definition of the term, and while fully aware of the dangers of collapse and chaos and the possibility of Communism that will accompany them, we heartily dislike the apparently suppressive aspects of the role we find we sometimes have to play.

This feeling is entirely natural and proper, but it is probably heightened by the oversimplified nature of much of our national folklore in which the heroes and villains cannot possibly be confused. Thousands of western tales and movies have shown us honest sheriffs and cowboys sporting gleaming white hats, riding white horses, and ultimately winning out over wicked train robbers, rustlers, and cardsharps, who are all suitably garbed in sinister black. The winners are all pure of heart and superbly confident of their own abilities and the rightness of their actions.

It may be more than coincidence that the "adult western" began to appear on the nation's screens at about the time the American people as a whole were becoming aware of the burdens of world leadership and the complexities of cold and unconventional war. The new-style hero is still victorious in the end, but his hat has changed to a battered brown or gray, he walks rather more than he rides, and he occasionally has very human doubts about his methods, his motives, and his judgment.

These qualms about unconventional warfare are relatively new for the American people as a whole, but they are nothing new to the men who do the fighting. During the Philippine insurrection of sixty years ago, the American volunteer soldier carrying his Krag-Jörgensen rifle through the jungle caught something of the same spirit in his bitter little song that "beneath our starry flag we'll civilize 'em with a Krag." That conflict was a short-lived colonial war, and the subsequent American record in the Philippines makes one of the finer chapters in our history, but we sense enough parallels between the misgivings then and now to make us vaguely uneasy. And this uneasiness is not helped by the Communist propagandists' perpetual pounding on the theme that we are imperialists at heart.

Then too, there is the nagging realization that our past interventions to ease revolutionary situations have not always had very satisfactory long-term consequences. Having forced the Spanish withdrawal from Cuba in 1898, we made extensive efforts from 1899 to 1902, and again from 1906 to 1909, to get the infant Cuban Government on its feet. Together with European powers we moved forces into China at the time of the Boxer Rebellion of 1900, and maintained troops there until the start of World War II. We joined our World War I associates in intervention in Russia and Manchuria from 1918 to 1920 in an effort to prevent the Communists from consolidating their power, and for over twenty years of this century U. S. Marines have been in Haiti trying to create the minimum conditions of order which might permit the growth of stable government. Our intervention in northern Mexico in 1915 was certainly not a success, and although other moves into Nicaragua and Guatemala had happier immediate results, they established an atmosphere in our relations with Latin America which our diplomats are still striving to improve. Even the solid achievement of building the Panama Canal has had unfortunate political echoes and, taken all in all, the intervention batting average has not been a very good one.

Not unnaturally these memories give us reason for pause as we contemplate the demands that are inevitably going to be placed upon us over the coming years. Any long-term policy which assumes the extended expenditure of large amounts of money and the inevitable loss of American lives is bound to evoke as much sharp emotional reaction as sober thought, and the policy of checking Communist expansion by countering unconventional aggression and contrived insurrections does all these.

At the danger of seeming to mouth truisms it is fair to say that our greatest needs over the next decade will be realism, patience, and sustained initiative. No realistic man can size up the state of the world today and conclude that the conduct of American affairs is going to be either simple or easy, and the temptation is great to seek out and seize some plausible panaceas that will somehow bring us victory on our own terms. The "don't just stand there, do something!" pressure that an uninformed and unrealistic public opinion can build up against the leaders of a democracy may lead to catastrophe unless both the leaders and the people know what they are doing.

Of course, this is related to the need for patience. It is hard for us to accept the fact that in countering unconventional aggression we may defeat our own objectives by applying too much pressure or the wrong sort of force, and so counterinsurgency in the underdeveloped countries becomes particularly trying. We can only move toward what amounts to victory at a pace limited and determined by the pace at which the country fighting off unconventional aggression can move toward political and economic stability. This, as we have seen, involves a process of social maturing which can be helped along but not rushed or bypassed.

Many of our greatest accomplishments, civil and military, have been pushed through on the old motto that "The difficult we do at once, the impossible takes a bit longer." Now we are facing a job that will absorb a significant amount of our national energy where the difficult is bound to take quite a while to do.

Few things are as numbing as a long-extended, uncongenial task; hence our need for sustained initiative to assure that we are protecting our security against the Communist form of aggression as effectively and as economically as we can. New opportunities for improved performance may always appear as time passes, but certainly the first job is to see that we are well organized for the task at hand.

As far as the United States is concerned, the military aspects of counterinsurgency operations call for flexible and highly professional forces. Massive citizen armies raised through large-scale mobilization are woefully expensive and can play no useful role in conflicts where political considerations demand that indigenous troops carry the main weight of the fighting. Large American reserves will obviously be needed in any struggle which escalates into a conventional war, but they have little or no direct application in the sort of conflict we are considering.

The need is rather for specialized troops, a high proportion of them with technical skills, to train and supplement the forces of the threatened states. American soldiers and marines now serving and fighting in South Vietnam and the Army and Marine Corps units that moved to the Mekong border of Thailand during the Laotian crisis of 1962 demonstrate that the Armed Forces are aware of the need and can act to meet it.

Indeed, the greatest difficulty in preparing the nation's military forces for this work may well be the doubts and reservations of the civilian population. In part, the problem is again one of changing traditions.

When the punitive expedition against Pancho Villa in northern Mexico ingloriously bogged down in 1916, the American Regular Army closed a period of nearly one hundred and fifty years during which one or more of its units had almost always been actively fighting against some irregularly organized enemy. The Philippine insurrection and the Moro campaign had followed more than a century of Indian fighting on the advancing western frontier. During that whole period a man enlisting in the Army knew that he was likely to see active field service, and he assumed the chances of battle in the same way a man joining a police or fire department assumes his chances with armed criminals or falling walls. Then in the inactive period after World War I, the public came to view service in the Army as a caretaker function. Regulars would train and lead their fellow citizens in event of war, but otherwise they were generally considered men of peace. Events in the Caribbean kept the Marines on a more publicly active footing, but the whole public concept of the military changed to that of a stand-by body.

The Korean conflict and the present extensive overseas commitments have tended to change this notion, and the exigencies of unconventional aggressions are now forcing us to revive the older concept of the regular military as an often active combat force.

It is clear today that we need to have a suitable segment of our armed might designed, equipped, and professionally trained to fight limited counterinsurgency campaigns through to what may be limited conclusions in support of long-term political and economic objectives. It is equally clear that the American people must be aware of the need for such forces and reconciled to the human and material costs of supporting them.

The civil aspects of our organizing to conduct effective counterinsurgency operations are certainly as important as the military, but they are hardly likely to arouse the same public interest and concern. Many steps have already been taken to improve our performance here. The fragmented activities of our embassies and military missions are being drawn closer together in those countries where unconventional aggression either threatens or is underway. The authority of the American ambassador on the spot has been strengthened to assure more effective management of the United States effort and to check free-wheeling and competitive activities. This is all to the good, but much remains to be done. Many specialists attached to missions in troubled areas still have the vexing problem of responding to two chiefs who are not always in full agreement—one being the ambassador, and the other a dim departmental figure at the end of the cable in Washington. Then too, some ambassadors and their immediate staffs are not yet sufficiently familiar with the hodgepodge of American activities in their areas to get the most out of each of them.

The interworking of American military and civilian activities is a complicated matter in itself, and while fortunately the personal relationships are usually cordial, the arrangements can be ponderous. For example, in areas where American troops are stationed, the military commander must work closely with the ambassador and receive much of his guidance from him. But the commander also takes his orders from the military theater commander, who may be a long ways away. The theater commander reports in turn to the Joint Chiefs of Staff in the Pentagon, and hence, his links with the ambassador to one of the nations in his area of military responsibility are fairly roundabout.

It is only fair to note, however, that by 1962 the Foreign Service, the Civil Service, and the military were rapidly coming to understand the role that each has to play in meeting this particular threat, and this understanding is dispelling much of the confusion and rivalry which has hampered a joint effort in the past.

In Washington similar adjustments are necessary to meet the special needs of counterinsurgency. Here too, changes are being made, but the organizational problems are more subtle and complicated than in the field. While many departments and agencies are involved in the work of countering unconventional aggression, this is but one of their varied tasks, and sweeping shifts or concentrations of authority have to be carefully planned, or they will only confuse and cripple other activities.

The time-honored but cumbersome solution to the difficulties that arise when different departments must work jointly on a matter or find that their authorities and responsibilities are overlapping is to set up special committees to coordinate the effort. Such committees come and go in a bureaucracy like summer flowers in a garden, and counterinsurgency has brought forth some fine ones. To an outside observer, these seem to be working unusually well. By their very nature, however, interdepartmental committees absorb an inordinate amount of the time of senior officials who have other duties to perform, and the committee staffs are rarely adequate to assure that decisions reached are carried through to execution.

Problems arising from unrest and insurrection in the lesser developed areas are going to be with us for a long time to come. Sooner or later the government will have to work out some permanent and more streamlined arrangement for reviewing and meeting them if important aspects of American planning and action are not to be overlooked or lost in the shuffle.

The need for a more efficient approach to these matters is also evident in the legislative process. As we have seen, effective counterinsurgency activity is a complex blending of military, political, and economic effort, and the Congress appropriates the money that makes the effort possible. Congress considers and approves the appropriations for the different but closely related elements of this effort entirely separately, and the size of many of the component parts is argued out and determined by separate committees. Because of the variety of the programs that have to be considered and the approach taken to them, an outside observer sometimes feels that Congress acts in these matters rather like a small boy working his way through an orchard. The most spectacularly attractive plums are quickly picked and approved. The less appealing ones are taken in slowly and after prolonged examination, and the remainder are ignored, rejected, or gathered reluctantly as a matter of duty.

To a great extent the actions of the members of Congress naturally and properly reflect the thoughts and wishes of the constituents these men represent, and it is probably evidence of the basic soundness of the system that the widely differing appropriations necessary for effective counterinsurgency operations come through the process with as few imbalances as they do. Still there is room for vast improvement. An adequate foreign information program, a perennial victim of the congressional ax, is often just as important for this work as the purchase of military hardware.

This brings us back to the critically important need for Americans to understand the nature of insurrectionary, unconventional warfare and its significance in today's world. If this understanding is achieved there is every prospect that the government will be able to concentrate its assets effectively and that the people will provide the needed backing and support. Then we will have good reason to believe that over the next decade the avowed Communist strategy of inciting and aiding "wars of national liberation" can be checked and defeated. We will be able to work effectively with the governments of the states under attack and, as the work progresses, will be able to bring more free nations into what must finally be a wide cooperative effort.

There are few things more important to us than to see this campaign successfully carried through, for there are few things which will contribute more to our ultimate security than the stable and peaceful development of the emergent nations of the world.

Suggested Reading

The following list of books and articles is not a bibliography, nor does it purport to be an inclusive listing of the ever-increasing body of literature concerned with irregular warfare and related topics. This relatively brief selection has been made for its possible use to interested readers who may wish to follow up some particular aspect of the subject.

Some of these books are devoted to irregular war in some specific part of the world. Those by Fall, Gillespie, Pye, and Tanham are examples. Amery and Dixon concern themselves with irregular operations in time of general war. The works by Giap, Guevara, Lawrence, and Mao are both personal memoirs and presentations of doctrine, while Rostow's *The Stages of Economic Growth* is not concerned with unconventional war at all, but rather describes the economic transitions and hurdles that often create the tensions leading to political instability.

Each of these works will broaden the reader's understanding of the nature and context of modern unconventional war.

Amery, Julian. *Sons of the Eagle: A Study in Guerilla War.* London: Macmillan & Co., 1948.
———. "Of Resistance" (article), *The Nineteenth Century and After,* March 1949.

Brinton, Crane. *The Anatomy of Revolution.* New York: W. W. Norton & Company, 1938; Revised Edition, New York: Prentice-Hall, 1952.

Chorley, Catharine C. *Armies and the Art of Revolution.* London: Faber & Faber, 1943.

Crozier, Brian. *The Rebels: A Study of Post-War Insurrections.* Boston: Beacon Press, 1960.

Dixon, Brigadier C. Aubrey, and Heilbrunn, Otto. *Communist Guerilla Warfare.* New York: Frederick A. Praeger, 1954.

Fall, Bernard B. *Street without Joy: Indochina at War, 1946–54.* Harrisburg, Pa.: The Stackpole Co., 1961.

Giap, General Vo Nguyen. *People's War, People's Army: The Viet Cong Insurrection Manual for Underdeveloped Countries.* Hanoi, North Vietnam: Foreign Languages Publishing House, 1961; New York: Frederick A. Praeger, 1962.

Gillespie, Joan. *Algeria: Rebellion and Revolution.* New York: Frederick A. Praeger, 1961.

Griffith, Brigadier General Samuel B., USMC (Ret.). *Mao Tse-tung on Guerrilla Warfare.* New York: Frederick A. Praeger, 1961.

Guevara, (Ernesto) Che. *Che Guevara on Guerrilla Warfare.* New York: Frederick A. Praeger, 1961.

————. Guerrilla Warfare (translated by J. P. Morray). New York: Monthly Review Press, 1961.

Heilbrunn, Otto. *Partisan Warfare.* New York: Frederick A. Praeger, 1962.

Lawrence, T. E. "Evolution of a Revolt." First published in *The Army Quarterly,* No. 1, October 1920. Reprinted in *Oriental Assembly* (edited by A. W. Lawrence). London: Williams & Norgate, 1939. Reprinted in part in *The Essential T. E. Lawrence,* selected and with a preface by David Garnett. London: Jonathan Cape, 1951. Sections of this article were later used in Chapter 33 of Lawrence's *Seven Pillars of Wisdom.*

Lindsay, Franklin A. "Unconventional Warfare," *Foreign Affairs,* January 1962.

Mao Tse-tung. *Selected Works,* 4 vols. New York: International Publishers Co., 1954–56.

Osanka, Franklin Mark (editor). *Modern Guerrilla Warfare—Fighting Communist Guerrilla Movements, 1941–1961.* New York: The Free Press of Glencoe, 1962.

Paret, Peter, and Shy, John W. *Guerrillas in the 1960's*. New York: Frederick A. Praeger, 1962.

Pye, Lucian W. *Guerrilla Communism in Malaya, Its Social and Political Meaning*. Princeton, N.J.: Princeton University Press, 1956.

———. *Politics, Personality, and Nation Building: Burma's Search for Identity*. New Haven, Conn.: Yale University Press, 1962.

Rostow, Walt W. Address to the graduating class at the U. S. Army Special Warfare School, Fort Bragg, N.C., June 28, 1961. The subject was American policy regarding guerrilla warfare in the underdeveloped areas. Under different titles slightly differing versions of this address have been published: *Army Magazine*, September 1961; *The Department of State Bulletin*, August 7, 1961; *Marine Corps Gazette*, January 1962; *Modern Guerrilla Warfare*, Franklin Mark Osanka, The Free Press of Glencoe, 1962, p. 464.

———. *The Stages of Economic Growth: A Non-Communist Manifesto*. New York: Cambridge University Press, 1960.

Tanham, George K. *Communist Revolutionary Warfare: The Vietminh in Indochina*. New York: Frederick A. Praeger, 1961.

Index